ROUND TWO

or New York in the Seventies

Eric Bentley

a Schnitzler variation

BROADWAY PLAY PUBLISHING INC
224 E 62nd St, NY, NY 10065
www.broadwayplaypub.com
info@broadwayplaypub.com

ROUND TWO
© Copyright 1990, 2008 by Eric Bentley

First printing: May 2008
I S B N: 0-88145-364-1

Book design: Marie Donovan
Word processing: Microsoft Word
Typographic controls: Ventura Publisher
Typeface: Palatino
Printed and bound in the U S A

CONTENTS

CHARACTERS

The Hustler
The Soldier
The Art Student
The Young Lawyer
The Businessman
The Lover
The Teenager
The Writer
The Actress
The V I P

ROUND TWO is dedicated to the memory of

Maxim Mazumdar

I wrote it for him to direct and play The Writer in.
He died, a victim of the great epidemic, in 1988.

Weltspiel, das herrische,
Mischt Sein und Schein—
Das Ewig-Närrische
Mischt uns—hinein!

Eternal Feminine
Gave us our cue
But time-bound Masculine
Was what we knew.
Into the quandary:
To seem or to be?
Eternal Foolery
Hurls you and me

1
The Hustler and the Soldier

(Times Square. The titles on the movie marquees are of the seventies. Late evening. Sidewalk. In the doorway of an adult bookstore, a Black HUSTLER *is standing. A very handsome* SOLDIER *walks by, smoking a cigar.)*

HUSTLER: *(In an undertone, close to the* SOLDIER's *ear)* Lookin' to score?

SOLDIER: Ha?

HUSTLER: You're gorgeous. Bargain rates for guys like you.

SOLDIER: You makin' a pass, faggot?

HUSTLER: Ladies' man, huh? *(Pause)* Takes all sorts to make a world.

*(*SOLDIER *turns away, looks in store window.)*

HUSTLER: Ten inches, ten bucks.

(Pause. SOLDIER *continues to study store window.)*

SOLDIER: Like, where?

HUSTLER: How 'bout your place?

SOLDIER: My place is Fort Dix.

HUSTLER: You stayin' in a hotel 'round here?

SOLDIER: Nah. Got no money anyhow.

HUSTLER: The army don't pay?

*(*SOLDIER *stares at him.)*

HUSTLER: I don't need no money.

SOLDIER: Oh, no? What's your racket? Coke?

HUSTLER: I gotta get money—from civilians. Not from guys in uniform.

SOLDIER: Patriotic, huh?

HUSTLER: You're gorgeous, Gorgeous.

SOLDIER: You're not bad lookin' yourself. How old are ya?

HUSTLER: Eighteen. You?

SOLDIER: Twenny-five.

HUSTLER: Perfect age! I'd like to be twenny-five for life.

SOLDIER: So where do we go?

HUSTLER: My place, I guess.

SOLDIER: Where's that?

HUSTLER: One thirty-fifth street.

SOLDIER: A hundred blocks away? Harlem at that. *(He again starts to go.)*

HUSTLER: My folks don't mind. *(Pause)* Lots of white guys like it there.

SOLDIER: I gotta get back to Fort Dix.

HUSTLER: How long you been in the army?

SOLDIER: Too long. How 'bout some place 'round here?

HUSTLER: Wanna pay for a hotel?

SOLDIER: Nah.

HUSTLER: Tell you what. Come tomorrah. Uptown. I'll give you the address.

SOLDIER: Now that shows real trust, don't it? *If* the address is correct. Okay, give it to me.

(HUSTLER does not.)

HUSTLER: You'll be a no show.

SOLDIER: So some white guys *don't* like it?

HUSTLER: There's a no show once in a while.

SOLDIER: I said okay.

HUSTLER: Tell you what. There's a place on Eighth Avenue.

SOLDIER: What street?

HUSTLER: 44th. Two blocks from here. Come to the corner, I'll show ya.

(They walk, then stop. HUSTLER points.)

HUSTLER: There!

SOLDIER: How d'we get in?

HUSTLER: The street door's open.

SOLDIER: And then?

HUSTLER: I'll show ya.

(Again, they walk.)

SOLDIER: *(As they enter a dimly lit building)* Can't see a fuckin' thing.

HUSTLER: Hold on to me, there's no rail on the stairs.

SOLDIER: If I'm dead, I'm dead.

HUSTLER: You're real morbid.

SOLDIER: Kill or get killed. That's war.

HUSTLER: Everythin's gonna be okay. I love ya, know what I mean?

SOLDIER: No. What?

HUSTLER: You remind me of someone.

SOLDIER: I heard that before someplace.

HUSTLER: I could use someone like you. For a boyfriend. A real lover!

SOLDIER: I'd make you too jealous.

HUSTLER: I could handle that.

SOLDIER: Think so, ha?

HUSTLER: Keep your voice down.

SOLDIER: Who would be in here?

HUSTLER: We don't wanna meet *nobody*, that's the thing.

SOLDIER: Okay, let's do it, let's do it.

HUSTLER: There's a better place next floor up. That floor got a railing.

SOLDIER: *(Pushing his groin out)* Feel this.

HUSTLER: My God, you're hard as iron. But if we do it here, you're gonna fall right off.

SOLDIER: *(Pushing* HUSTLER *down on his knees)* Get goin', get goin'.

HUSTLER: Against the wall then. Lean back against the wall.

(SOLDIER *does so.)*

* * * * *

HUSTLER: We shoulda gone up on the next floor.

SOLDIER: *(Buttoning his fiy)* One floor's like another. When are you gonna get up?

HUSTLER: There's no rush. Lemme—

SOLDIER: Gotta get back to Fort Dix. I'm late awready.

HUSTLER: *(Getting up)* What's your name, baby?

SOLDIER: Whadda you want my name for?

HUSTLER: Because I love ya, remember? I'll tell you mine: Hyacinth.

SOLDIER: A fuckin' flower.

HUSTLER: Anyway, George—you look like a George

SOLDIER: Anyway, what? And *I'm* not a George!

HUSTLER: I seen your I D.

SOLDIER: Sly, huh? Suppose it's not *my* I D?

HUSTLER: Can you loan me ten bucks?

SOLDIER: What d'ya think I am? So long. *(He starts off down the stairs.)*

HUSTLER: *(Quietly)* Cunt! Motherfucker!

2
The Soldier and the Art Student

(Night. On the sidewalk outside the Underground, a disco near Union Square. The SOLDIER is pulling the ART STUDENT out of the disco. Seventies disco music is heard throughout the scene.)

ART STUDENT: Why did you keep wanting to leave?

(The SOLDIER gives an embarrassed laugh.)

ART STUDENT: Don't you like to dance?

SOLDIER: *(Holding him close, and slow-dancing to the music)* Sure.

ART STUDENT: This is not dancing, it's sex.

SOLDIER: *(Stopping the dance)* I don't even know your name. Did someone in there call you Kevin?

ART STUDENT: So there was a Kevin caught your eye?

SOLDIER: Okay, that was *him.* They called you—Desmond?

ART STUDENT: This is a dangerous block. Full of fag bashers.

SOLDIER: You're under the protection of the armed forces, Desmond!

(He pulls the ART STUDENT *with him along the block.)*

ART STUDENT: Where are we going? I can't see an inch in front of my nose.

SOLDIER: *(Using a cigarette lighter)* How 'bout now?

ART STUDENT: You're a looker, aren't you?

SOLDIER: You like me?

ART STUDENT: You were the best looking guy in the whole place.

SOLDIER: You're not bad yourself.

ART STUDENT: But Kevin was the one you danced with most of the time.

SOLDIER: That's because I knew him awready.

ART STUDENT: And you thought I was Kevin?

SOLDIER: I was just kiddin'. Did you see my buddy?

ART STUDENT: The other guy in uniform?

SOLDIER: Yeah. Kevin's dancin' with him.

ART STUDENT: He's pretty fresh. The other guy in uniform.

SOLDIER: Did he try somethin' on you? I told him you were *my* property.

ART STUDENT: Well, he didn't listen. And I'm not your property.

SOLDIER: Hey, look, I meant that as a compliment.

ART STUDENT: United States property. I'm honored. Maybe.

SOLDIER: And I knew you were Desmond.

ART STUDENT: You don't have a name?

SOLDIER: Top secret.

ART STUDENT: I'm going back in.

SOLDIER: *(Stopping him)* My name's George.

ART STUDENT: As in Washington. I like that.

SOLDIER: So keep movin'.

(They do so.)

ART STUDENT: Can't see a thing. *(It's dark but he sees something.)* Hey, no. They're not doin' it right there, are they? In the parking lot?

SOLDIER: *(Pointing to another section of the lot)* And that?

ART STUDENT: *(Seeing something else)* My God, it's an orgy.

SOLDIER: Nah. They mind their own business.

ART STUDENT: Let's go back.

SOLDIER: Lemme touch you first. Just lemme touch ya.

(ART STUDENT allows SOLDIER to touch him.)

ART STUDENT: My God but not like that. My God. We're still on the sidewalk.

SOLDIER: *(Pulling him into the darkness)* Not here we're not.

* * * * *

(ART STUDENT steps into the light of the streetlamp.)

SOLDIER: *(From the dark)* Hey, where you goin'?

ART STUDENT: That was great.

SOLDIER: So where you goin'?

ART STUDENT: Back in, I guess. Where are you?

SOLDIER: Waitin' for you.

ART STUDENT: You wanna do it again? Right away?

SOLDIER: Come— See.

(ART STUDENT *hesitates.*)

SOLDIER: Come— See.

(ART STUDENT *moves back into the darkness.*)

＊ ＊ ＊ ＊ ＊

(SOLDIER *steps into the light of the streetlamp.*)

SOLDIER: You're the affectionate type.

ART STUDENT: (*Following him eagerly*) That was real nice.

SOLDIER: Let's get back in there.

ART STUDENT: (*Trying to embrace him*) What's the hurry?

(SOLDIER *pulls away.*)

ART STUDENT: Why d'ya walk away?

SOLDIER: To get this damn cigar lit. (*He gets his cigar lit and enjoys the first puff.*)

ART STUDENT: (*Hurt*) You like cigars, huh? D'you like me?

SOLDIER: (*Laughs*) Three guesses! Let's get back in there.

ART STUDENT: Why?

SOLDIER: And why stick around in a parking lot, for God's sake? This is a rough block.

ART STUDENT: Do you *like* me?

SOLDIER: I picked you, didn't I? I haven't had sex with no one else, have I?

ART STUDENT: Then hold me in your arms.

SOLDIER: Okay. (*As he takes hold of him, the music comes up louder.*) Just listen to the music!

ART STUDENT: You'd rather dance?

SOLDIER: Yeah. Let's get back in.

ART STUDENT: I'm gonna have to leave. I've an exam tomorrow.

SOLDIER: Where at?

ART STUDENT: Parson's School of Design.

SOLDIER: Sounds like it has "class". Design, huh?

ART STUDENT: Will you walk me to the subway? This section's dangerous.

SOLDIER: Where's the nearest stop?

ART STUDENT: Union Square.

SOLDIER: Oh, that's on my way.... But not now. I got a late pass at Dix. Come back in for a while.

ART STUDENT: Kevin's in there, isn't he?

SOLDIER: The jealousy bit!

ART STUDENT: So it *is* Kevin.

SOLDIER: Bullshit.

ART STUDENT: Okay, dance all night with *me*, and I'll come back in!

(The music has stopped. A new tune starts here.)

SOLDIER: Hear that? This I can't miss. *(He sings along for a bar or two.)* Okay, I'll walk you to Union Square. Later. If you wanna wait. If not, goo' night.

ART STUDENT: Good night. No, wait a minute, George. Okay, I'll wait.

SOLDIER: Get yourself a drink, Desmond. Or something stronger. I'll pick you up at the bar.

ART STUDENT: *(Left alone)* So I'm an M. As in S and M. But he *is* gorgeous.

3
The Art Student and the Young Lawyer

(Warm summer afternoon. An Upper East Side apartment. In the bedroom he gets in return for houseboy services, the ART STUDENT, *in a cotton sweater and short shorts , sits writing a letter to the* SOLDIER.

ART STUDENT: *(Reading)* 'Dearest George: how is Dix? No, I did *not* say, How *are* Dix! I enclose five high quality cigars. Crumbs from the rich man's table. The rich man's my new boss, a lawyer. Works out of his apartment where yours truly is houseboy. Strictly professional, of course. I answered his ad in the *Village Voice.* He's gay, but the ad said, in so many words, "This is not a sex ad" and anyway, George, I'm yours now.
I dream of your bod:
It rhymes with God.
Poetry! Your lover to all eternity and keep your hands off that Private First Class, Desmond.'

(A buzzer rings. The ART STUDENT *gets up and goes to the next room, the living room, where the* YOUNG LAWYER, *in shirt sleeves and slacks, is busy mastering his new word processor.)*

ART STUDENT: You buzzed?

YOUNG LAWYER: Did I? Oh yes. Desmond, right? Now what was it? Oh yes, would you help me with the Venetian blinds. I can't get them to come down.

(ART STUDENT lowers the blinds, which present no problem.)

YOUNG LAWYER: Well, thanks.

ART STUDENT: Is that a computer?

(He looks over YOUNG LAWYER's shoulder.)

YOUNG LAWYER: I B M Composer. Computer with a word processing program. An invention that makes the seventies, the seventies.

(ART STUDENT *leaves.* YOUNG LAWYER *works away at word processing. Then presses a button, and the buzzer rings in* ART STUDENT's *room.* ART STUDENT *returns.)*

ART STUDENT: Yes?

YOUNG LAWYER: Oh, Desmond, yes, *(Again he has been interrupted at work)* is there any brandy—in the liquor cabinet?

ART STUDENT: Let's see. *(The cabinet is near the word processor.)* No. No liquor at all.

YOUNG LAWYER: Oh, well, you'd better leave me to it.

(ART STUDENT *leaves. Same business)*

ART STUDENT: Yes?

YOUNG LAWYER: Get me some iced water, would you?

ART STUDENT: *(Looking in the icebox)* There's some in the icebox. Where shall I put it?

YOUNG LAWYER: Give it to me.

(Their fingers touch on the glass. For a split second they make eye contact.)

YOUNG LAWYER: Well, well, I *must* get on with this.

(ART STUDENT *withdraws.* YOUNG LAWYER *works on briefly, then buzzes.)*

ART STUDENT: *(Minus his sweater. He is wearing a pink tank top)* Here I am.

YOUNG LAWYER: Again? Oh yes. I keep forgetting why I buzzed you in the first place.

ART STUDENT: Why *was* that?

YOUNG LAWYER: Oh yes, to say I was expecting someone. To give me my lesson. How to use this thing. *(He points to the processor.)*

ART STUDENT: I didn't know lawyers used computers.

YOUNG LAWYER: They use secretaries. This miracle of modern science will save me all those salaries... The guy's name is Schuller. He should've been here long ago.

ART STUDENT: I see.

YOUNG LAWYER: He hasn't been here already, has he?

ART STUDENT: No.

YOUNG LAWYER: Are you sure? Would you know him?

ART STUDENT: No one has been by. *(Lingering in the doorway)* Shall I go now, sir?

YOUNG LAWYER: Yes. No. Desmond, about that "sir" business. This is not the Victorian age. Didn't I tell you to call me Alex?

ART STUDENT: No, but I will...Alex.

YOUNG LAWYER: This is your third day, isn't it? I must've said something about it?

ART STUDENT: Well, we haven't really talked since you interviewed me for the job.

YOUNG LAWYER: And I didn't say: call me Alex?

ART STUDENT: No. You just said, let's keep this professionally correct.

YOUNG LAWYER: Is that how I put it?

ART STUDENT: In the *Village Voice* you said: "This is not a sex ad." It just happened, you explained later, that you didn't really want a girl on the premises.

YOUNG LAWYER: Too much responsibility. In New York.

ART STUDENT: Is there something else I should've remembered?

YOUNG LAWYER: No, that's about it. Sex on the job is a mess. So, since we're both grown men... *(He stops.)*

ART STUDENT: Yes?

YOUNG LAWYER: Well, you get the general idea.

(Pause. YOUNG LAWYER *still tinkering with the machine,* ART STUDENT *lingering.)*

YOUNG LAWYER: Look, Desmond, are you flirting with me?

ART STUDENT: Flirting?

YOUNG LAWYER: How about that shirt?

ART STUDENT: Too pink?

YOUNG LAWYER: You *are* gay, aren't you?

ART STUDENT: "This is not a sex ad."

YOUNG LAWYER: I know you *are.*

ART STUDENT: Do I hide it?

YOUNG LAWYER: I don't mean that. I mean there are men in your life.

ART STUDENT: Men, plural?

YOUNG LAWYER: Or man, singular.

ART STUDENT: Do you peep through keyholes, Alex?

YOUNG LAWYER: No, you leave doors open, Desmond.

ART STUDENT: That door of yours is not *left* open. It will not close.

YOUNG LAWYER: I saw what I saw.

ART STUDENT: You're a voyeur, Alex!

YOUNG LAWYER: And what are you?

ART STUDENT: Me?

YOUNG LAWYER: You're staying. In *my* room.

ART STUDENT: You don't want me to?

YOUNG LAWYER: Well, Desmond, I should confess this: *I'm* gay.

ART STUDENT: That's cool.

YOUNG LAWYER: And I find you...shall I say attractive?

ART STUDENT: I think you shall. And, gee, thanks.

YOUNG LAWYER: You're still there.

ART STUDENT: Should I leave?

YOUNG LAWYER: Yes.

(ART STUDENT *starts to do so.*)

YOUNG LAWYER: Desmond!

ART STUDENT: *(Turning)* Yes, Alex?

YOUNG LAWYER: Who was the guy?

ART STUDENT: The guy?

YOUNG LAWYER: I saw him. With my own eyes.

ART STUDENT: Ah yes, Alex, the voyeur. Who saw what he saw.

YOUNG LAWYER: You and—

ART STUDENT: *(Firmly)* My lover, Alex. That was my lover.

YOUNG LAWYER: You have a lover? You're going steady!

ART STUDENT: And that's wrong?

YOUNG LAWYER: No, no, I like couples very much. And of course they should be faithful.

ART STUDENT: And you are a single, Alex?

YOUNG LAWYER: *(Nodding)* Not for the world would I break up a couple. The world is my Singles Bar.

ART STUDENT: You *confine* yourself to singles?

YOUNG LAWYER: *(Nodding again)* And the occasional double.

ART STUDENT: You go in for threesomes?

YOUNG LAWYER: No, no, no. Desmond! Don't you recall what someone or other said about marriage?

ART STUDENT: I'm not too familiar with someone or other.

YOUNG LAWYER: Marriage is a cage: those who are in want to get out, those who are out want to get in.

ART STUDENT: And you enjoy catching those who want to get out!

YOUNG LAWYER: How did you guess?

ART STUDENT: The way you said: You have a lover?

YOUNG LAWYER: How *did* I say it?

ART STUDENT: Like it was very much your business.

YOUNG LAWYER: I shouldn't love my fellow men?

ART STUDENT: Do you love your fellow women?

YOUNG LAWYER: Desmond, you *are* flirting with me.

ART STUDENT: No, I'm not.

YOUNG LAWYER: The pink tank top. The hanging around. The way you look at me.

ART STUDENT: My heart belongs to another. I told you that.

YOUNG LAWYER: Then why did you remove your sweater?

ART STUDENT: I was too warm. *(Pause)* And I thought you could take it in your stride.

YOUNG LAWYER: Desmond, you may leave.

ART STUDENT: I know that. *(Pause)* I know I may leave.

YOUNG LAWYER: Then do it for God's sake.

ART STUDENT: You mean: do it or else?

YOUNG LAWYER: Yes, do it. Or else.

ART STUDENT: Or else what?

YOUNG LAWYER: Or else! ...I may do something I'll regret later.

ART STUDENT: As long as it's not something *I'll* regret later.

YOUNG LAWYER: Huh? But you would. You'd feel all the guilt of...adultery.

ART STUDENT: How d'you know?

YOUNG LAWYER: This all began with you declaring you had a lover.

ART STUDENT: This all began with you watching me make love.

YOUNG LAWYER: Then you repeatedly said your heart belonged to another.

ART STUDENT: I said that *once*. Besides...

YOUNG LAWYER: Ah, so there's a "besides"?

ART STUDENT: It wasn't my heart you saw through that open door.

YOUNG LAWYER: Now you *are* making a pass. Desmond, you have me totally confused.

ART STUDENT: You've never heard of an open relationship?

YOUNG LAWYER: Huh? What's that?

ART STUDENT: George and I have an open relationship.

YOUNG LAWYER: I'm losing my self control. *(Silence)*
And you're not going to your room. *(Silence)* Desmond,
if this keeps up, I just may break the rules.

ART STUDENT: "Oh, sir!"

YOUNG LAWYER: Oh, Alex.

*(*YOUNG LAWYER *moves across the room and removes* ART
STUDENT's *tank top:* ART STUDENT *calmly lets him do so.)*

ART STUDENT: *(Continuing the talk)* Yes, of course:
"Alex". You're certainly Alex—now.

(They stand looking at one another.)

YOUNG LAWYER: You let me do it.

ART STUDENT: What if Mister Schuller rings the bell?

YOUNG LAWYER: Let him ring. He'll think I'm out.

ART STUDENT: *(Gently)* Now I don't want to cause you—

YOUNG LAWYER: *(Fervently)* Oh please, please—

* * * * *

*(The door bell is ringing. They are getting their clothes back
on.)*

YOUNG LAWYER: Jesus Christ, he'll rouse the whole
neighborhood! D'you think he was ringing all along
and we just didn't hear?

ART STUDENT: No, no, I was listening for him.

YOUNG LAWYER: Look through the peephole.

ART STUDENT: I just wanted to say: I like you, Alex.

YOUNG LAWYER: Please, go!

*(*ART STUDENT *goes.* YOUNG LAWYER *pulls the blinds up.
Light floods in.)*

ART STUDENT: *(At the peephole)* No one there now,
but I suppose it was Mister Schuller.

YOUNG LAWYER: Thanks. That's all for now—Desmond.

ART STUDENT: What!?

YOUNG LAWYER: I told you from the first. That was *not*
a sex ad. Besides—

ART STUDENT: Now *you* have a "besides"—?

YOUNG LAWYER: *(Severely)*. You have a relationship.

ART STUDENT: An open relationship. And...not as close
as I made out...I've only seen George once and it wasn't
George *you* saw, it was David, and I only saw *him*
once—

YOUNG LAWYER: *(Still severe)* That is none of my
business. I don't break up relationships whatever
they are!

ART STUDENT: *(Crestfallen)* I'd like to...make a
relationship...with you.

YOUNG LAWYER: Desmond! I have made a fool of
myself and I apologize. Now, all will be as it was.

ART STUDENT: Ha? I *can* keep the job?

YOUNG LAWYER: Just keep to the job. Your job. And I'll
keep to mine. Oh, Desmond, I'm really sorry about this.
(Silence) But, look, I did say: that will be all.

ART STUDENT: You're not consistent...Alex.

YOUNG LAWYER: I was right the first time. Our
relationship is going to be entirely correct from now on.

ART STUDENT: But—

(The bell starts ringing again.)

YOUNG LAWYER: Desmond, I am going to let Mister
Schuller in. Please go to your room!

(YOUNG LAWYER *leaves the room.* ART STUDENT *looks quickly about him, spots a cigar box, takes a handful of cigars and, shaking his head, goes back to his room.*)

4
The Young Lawyer and the Businessman

(The same setting as 3. When he has finished donning a business suit, YOUNG LAWYER *tidies up the living room so that it looks, when he's finished, like an office, dominated by the word processor. He places books and papers prominently. The bell rings. He lets in a young black man, also in a business suit.)*

YOUNG LAWYER: Michael!

BUSINESSMAN: Alex! *(They shake hands first, then switch to a cordial, slightly embarrassed embrace.)* Well, I came!

YOUNG LAWYER: I knew you would.

BUSINESSMAN: I told myself I wouldn't.

YOUNG LAWYER: And right on time too. Make yourself comfortable.

BUSINESSMAN: *(Sitting in the chair* YOUNG LAWYER *indicates)* Is this really your law office?

YOUNG LAWYER: Doesn't it look like it?

BUSINESSMAN: This is an apartment house. In a high-class residential neighborhood.

YOUNG LAWYER: *(Waving his hand around the room)* Law office. And that's a word processor.

(BUSINESSMAN *looks it over.*)

YOUNG LAWYER: America's new toy.

BUSINESSMAN: No bed?

YOUNG LAWYER: In a law office? Michael! Gin and tonic?

BUSINESSMAN: Thanks. It's funny, isn't it. Since we're both gay, you'd think—

YOUNG LAWYER: But—you're in a certain situation and I accept it.

BUSINESSMAN: A certain situation. Known as marriage. To a guy. D'you believe in gay marriages? We do.

YOUNG LAWYER: And I have to respect that fact. As I did when we talked.

BUSINESSMAN: Just like straights, gay people can be...just friends, after all.

(YOUNG LAWYER *hands* BUSINESSMAN *his drink.*)

BUSINESSMAN: Thanks.

YOUNG LAWYER: Not just 'after all' but, as you said, 'above all'. Cheers! *(They drink.)*

BUSINESSMAN: Cheers! Friends above all. And just friends.

YOUNG LAWYER: *(Sitting, now, to chat)* According to Plato, it's the greatest relationship there is, friendship. So we're denying ourselves nothing. We're even giving ourselves a present.

BUSINESSMAN: Don't make it sound like my lover is the unlucky one.

YOUNG LAWYER: He's lucky in his own way. We're lucky in ours.

BUSINESSMAN: Absolutely. That's why I'm here. To come here otherwise would be playing with fire.

YOUNG LAWYER: And no one would want to...play with fire.

BUSINESSMAN: Right. *(Pause)* One of your neighbors saw me ring your bell.

YOUNG LAWYER: Yes?

BUSINESSMAN: I hope he doesn't know Michael. My lover's called Michael, too.

YOUNG LAWYER: Michael and Michael! One of my neighbors might know you both, recognize one Michael, and report back to the other?

BUSINESSMAN: Yes.

YOUNG LAWYER: Report back what? That you rang a door bell?

BUSINESSMAN: He's very jealous. I mean he would be. If he had reason to be.

YOUNG LAWYER: But he hasn't. You're paranoid, Michael.

BUSINESSMAN: He has my promise. Absolute fidelity.

YOUNG LAWYER: You can't tell him someone's just a friend even when it's true?

BUSINESSMAN: Maybe I could. But I won't. For his sake. Don't want to bug him.

YOUNG LAWYER: So the just-friends-routine is for me only!

BUSINESSMAN: Just-friends-routine? It's the truth, isn't it?

YOUNG LAWYER: That's what I said. It's the truth. But just for me?

BUSINESSMAN: For the two of us.

(They both drink.)

BUSINESSMAN: It's hot in here.

YOUNG LAWYER: Take your coat off.

BUSINESSMAN: What? Oh, sure. *(He puts his jacket on the back of a chair and sits down again.)* Cheers!

YOUNG LAWYER: Cheers!

(They both drink. YOUNG LAWYER *kicks off his moccasins.)*

YOUNG LAWYER: Take your shoes off, Michael!
Be comfortable!

*(*BUSINESSMAN *looks dubious.)*

YOUNG LAWYER: Among friends? *(Pause)* In Japan
they all take their shoes off.

*(*BUSINESSMAN *kicks off his moccasins.)*

BUSINESSMAN: I must leave.

YOUNG LAWYER: In your socks?

BUSINESSMAN: Don't you remember, I finally agreed
to come to your office—if it is just your office—and
if we could just be friends—and if I could leave in five
minutes.

YOUNG LAWYER: Fine. All those conditions are met.
You *can* leave. Friends of mine are free to leave at any
time. This is America!

(Pause)

BUSINESSMAN: This room is stifling.

YOUNG LAWYER: You are wearing a vest.

*(*BUSINESSMAN *takes the vest off, places it on the jacket,
and sits again.)*

BUSINESSMAN: What time is it?

YOUNG LAWYER: You are also wearing a watch.

BUSINESSMAN: *(Consulting same)* Six o'clock on the nose.
I should've been at my sister's an hour ago. *(He stands.)*

YOUNG LAWYER: You can see your sister any time.

BUSINESSMAN: I must leave.

(*But* YOUNG LAWYER *has got up and gone to the door.*)

BUSINESSMAN: You are blocking the doorway!

YOUNG LAWYER: Ah, now we're getting somewhere.

BUSINESSMAN: (*Sitting again*) Alex, you are breaking your promise.

YOUNG LAWYER: Which one? You make me promise so many things!

BUSINESSMAN: Above all—

YOUNG LAWYER: And "after all"—

BUSINESSMAN: You promised to be good.

YOUNG LAWYER: Me and Queen Victoria.

BUSINESSMAN: You know what I mean.

YOUNG LAWYER: Queen Victoria knew what she meant. Finish your drink.

BUSINESSMAN: (*Picking up the glass*) Oh, God, Alex, why did you get me into this?

YOUNG LAWYER: (*Leaving the door*) D' you really wanna know?

BUSINESSMAN: Of course I do.

YOUNG LAWYER: (*Sitting facing* BUSINESSMAN *again, his own glass in hand*) Even though you know damn well what I'm gonna say.

BUSINESSMAN: I don't. I swear I don't.

YOUNG LAWYER: You're a liar, Michael. That should give *me* a certain license. But I'm not even lying. I *thought* it would be possible for us just to be friends. I was mistaken.

BUSINESSMAN: No!

YOUNG LAWYER: *(Singing)* Falling in love again, never wanted to...

BUSINESSMAN: No, no, we must keep love out of this—

YOUNG LAWYER: Ha? It's a deal. I'll settle for naked lust.

BUSINESSMAN: I can't bear it.

YOUNG LAWYER: Substitute a euphemism: lechery, lubricity, lasciviousness, debauchery, profligacy...

(BUSINESSMAN undoes buttons on his shirt.)

YOUNG LAWYER: It's *that* hot? I'll open a window. *(He gets up and does so.)*

BUSINESSMAN: Alex, Alex, you don't know me! I was going to be a priest. Till I met *him*. I was in the Seminary...

YOUNG LAWYER: Really? You need another drink. *(He pours another drink for both.)* Is it true that seminarians carry on something terrible?

BUSINESSMAN: *We* didn't.

YOUNG LAWYER: No orgies? No visits from Cardinal Spellman?

BUSINESSMAN: Alex, what I'm trying to tell you is: you and I only met yesterday.

YOUNG LAWYER: We only talked yesterday. We'd *met* before that.

BUSINESSMAN: Eye contact maybe. At the Opera.

YOUNG LAWYER: *(Ready with the drinks)* Cheers!

BUSINESSMAN: Only for a moment. Cheers!

YOUNG LAWYER: *(Seated again) Our* eyes had met even before that.

BUSINESSMAN: New York is all eyes!

YOUNG LAWYER: Eyes that *avoid* eye contact.

BUSINESSMAN: Eyes that stare hatred. At gays. At Blacks. Not to mention gay Blacks.

YOUNG LAWYER: Whereas we...you remember now?

BUSINESSMAN: *(Slowly)* In the Nickel Bar on West 72nd Street?

YOUNG LAWYER: You with your lily white lover. "Spouse" I should say. I could tell he was a spouse. He was between us, wasn't he?

BUSINESSMAN: You looked right across him.

YOUNG LAWYER: Man of distinction, your spouse. Silver hair. The Brooks Brothers look. What does he do?

BUSINESSMAN: He's in real estate. With me. Semi-retired. I do the work, he—

YOUNG LAWYER: Puts up the dough?

BUSINESSMAN: Alex!

YOUNG LAWYER: I'm only jealous. Where d'you live—Sutton Place?

BUSINESSMAN: We have a brownstone in Harlem.

YOUNG LAWYER: Oh, among the natives?

BUSINESSMAN: He has a thing for Blacks.

YOUNG LAWYER: Do you have a thing for Whites?

BUSINESSMAN: It's stifling in here.

*(*YOUNG LAWYER *jumps up to consult the thermostat.)*

BUSINESSMAN: Okay, I'm a snow queen.

YOUNG LAWYER: The temperature's down to sixty-five.

BUSINESSMAN: I gotta lie down.

YOUNG LAWYER: Lie down? Did you say lie down?

BUSINESSMAN: Yes. I gotta lie down.

YOUNG LAWYER: Great! The Big Lie can now be exposed. This *is* my apartment, Michael, and I *don't* sleep on the floor.

(He presses a button, and a wall bed descends swiftly from the wall to the floor. BUSINESSMAN *gasps.)*

YOUNG LAWYER: I even have a houseboy in the spare bedroom.

BUSINESSMAN: Have there been men in that bed before me?

YOUNG LAWYER: That bed has been there for years.

BUSINESSMAN: The wages of sin—

YOUNG LAWYER: Is death! You need to lie down.

(He beckons to BUSINESSMAN, *who allows himself to be placed on his back on the bed.)*

YOUNG LAWYER: Now close your eyes and listen to me.

(Hypnotized, BUSINESSMAN *does so .)*

YOUNG LAWYER: I lied to you—on one small point— to make one big point clear: you turn me on.

*(*BUSINESSMAN *opens his eyes in panic.)*

YOUNG LAWYER: Close your eyes.

*(*BUSINESSMAN *does so.)*

YOUNG LAWYER: Be glad that you have that effect on people. On this person. Ten years from now you won't. "For faggots are as roses whose fair flower/Being once displayed doth fade that very hour."

BUSINESSMAN: *(With eyes closed)* The way you put things.

YOUNG LAWYER: Close your eyes.

BUSINESSMAN: I'm shivering now.

YOUNG LAWYER: *(Starts to take his clothes off)* I'm going to warm you up.

* * * * *

(Both are in bed unclothed.)

YOUNG LAWYER: Now, how did *that* happen?

BUSINESSMAN: You couldn't get it up, Alex.

YOUNG LAWYER: I know I couldn't get it up, Michael.
I asked how did it happen.

BUSINESSMAN: It happens to the best of people
sometimes.

YOUNG LAWYER: It doesn't bother you?

BUSINESSMAN: It should bother *me*? I came.

YOUNG LAWYER: Bitch. Okay. Now tell your friendly
New York Post reporter how it feels to be an adulterer.

BUSINESSMAN: Super-bitch. But then I *was* bullshitting.
I've done this before, Alex. I mean, at least once.

YOUNG LAWYER: So now we get the truth. And I put
all that effort into—

BUSINESSMAN: Seducing me. I *had* to be seduced,
you see.

YOUNG LAWYER: By a eunuch?

BUSINESSMAN: Oh, come on. It did bother me—
that you were—

YOUNG LAWYER: Impotent.

BUSINESSMAN: Talking someone into sex is one thing,
Alex. Having sex is another.

YOUNG LAWYER: Yes, Daddy.

BUSINESSMAN: Active in one role, maybe you wanna
be passive in the other.

YOUNG LAWYER: My God, you've been reading those
ads in the gay papers: Top Man Wanted.

BUSINESSMAN: I'm not talking body. *I'm* talking soul.

YOUNG LAWYER: You want to be the active soul?

BUSINESSMAN: I'm saying you were hyper-active as seducer—

YOUNG LAWYER: And you were hyper-passive—

BUSINESSMAN: *(Shaking his head)* Just coy. To bring out the seducer in you.

YOUNG LAWYER: And if we switch roles—

BUSINESSMAN: Me active, you passive—maybe I'd warm *you* up.

(Silence. YOUNG LAWYER *just lies there.* BUSINESSMAN *takes him in his arms.)*

* * * * *

(They are getting dressed during this conversation.)

BUSINESSMAN: Maybe it takes a married man.

YOUNG LAWYER: A seminarian. That was sacramental sex. Holy communion.

BUSINESSMAN: Was it all right?

YOUNG LAWYER: It was an all-time high.

BUSINESSMAN: This time I *must* go.

YOUNG LAWYER: Oh, let your sister wait.

BUSINESSMAN: It's much too late for my sister's. I must go straight home.

YOUNG LAWYER: To *him*?

BUSINESSMAN: You're damn right. What time *is* it?

YOUNG LAWYER: The watch was all yours.

BUSINESSMAN: You took it off me. You took everything off me.

YOUNG LAWYER: *Touché.* *(Finding the watch)* Eight o'clock.

BUSINESSMAN: Eight o'clock! There'll be hell to pay.

YOUNG LAWYER: Not that you're gonna tell him?

BUSINESSMAN: But *what* am I gonna tell him?

YOUNG LAWYER: You got stuck in the Lexington Avenue subway.

BUSINESSMAN: He knows I don't use the subways. He won't *let* me use the subways.

YOUNG LAWYER: You'll think of something. You have a rich fantasy life.

BUSINESSMAN: How would *you* know?

YOUNG LAWYER: One lover, one spouse. When does your lover see you next?

BUSINESSMAN: Never!

YOUNG LAWYER: After that all-time high?

BUSINESSMAN: *Because* of that all-time high.

YOUNG LAWYER: Here's your shirt.

BUSINESSMAN: *(Shuddering)* This escapade could cost me my neck.

YOUNG LAWYER: Why?

BUSINESSMAN: He's gonna ask where I've been.

YOUNG LAWYER: You've been at your sister's, silly.

BUSINESSMAN: I'm a bad liar.

YOUNG LAWYER: Learn from your lover.

BUSINESSMAN: If only you were just a liar.

YOUNG LAWYER: What am I?

BUSINESSMAN: A bachelor. Probably sleeping with half
New York.

YOUNG LAWYER: Please!

BUSINESSMAN: At least with your houseboy. Houseboys
are bed boys.

YOUNG LAWYER: No sex. I put that in the ad.

BUSINESSMAN: *(Sighing)* Alex, what will it be like if, say,
ten years from now, we should meet again, you and
me? Bump into one another in an airport or someplace?

YOUNG LAWYER: Come off it. You'll be at the Nickel Bar
tomorrow night.

BUSINESSMAN: I will not.

YOUNG LAWYER: Then you'll be here. Day after
tomorrow.

BUSINESSMAN: What? Can't we discuss that—
at the Nickel Bar tomorrow?

YOUNG LAWYER: So you will be there.

BUSINESSMAN: But with *him.*

YOUNG LAWYER: That won't work.

BUSINESSMAN: How'd you like to be our lawyer? We
just about had it with old Lester, our present legal eagle.

YOUNG LAWYER: I' m not in real estate.

BUSINESSMAN: Be practical. I'm not about to leave
Michael for you.

YOUNG LAWYER: Spouse before lover every time.

BUSINESSMAN: Then again: how can one hold on to the
lover for a while without losing the spouse?

YOUNG LAWYER: Introduce lover to spouse as "our new
lawyer"?

BUSINESSMAN: Our *possible* new lawyer. Even if he says no, he'll have met you. From then on, you're family.

YOUNG LAWYER: Now wait a minute. This marriage of yours. You deceive him. So I suppose he deceives you?

BUSINESSMAN: He does *not*.

YOUNG LAWYER: Does he know about you?

BUSINESSMAN: Of course not.

YOUNG LAWYER: Then how do you know about him?

BUSINESSMAN: I know him, that's all. Through and through. He wants to settle down, and he *has* settled down.

YOUNG LAWYER: But does he thinkyou wanna settle down?

BUSINESSMAN: Obviously he does.

YOUNG LAWYER: Then he's stupid. Only men over fifty settle down.

BUSINESSMAN: Maybe he doesn't know that.

YOUNG LAWYER: Or maybe it's you that's stupid, and he has you good and fooled.

BUSINESSMAN: Ha?

YOUNG LAWYER: Maybe he does know about you.

BUSINESSMAN: If he did, he'd raise Cain.

YOUNG LAWYER: If he could afford to. But if he couldn't?

BUSINESSMAN: He'd *pretend* not to know.

YOUNG LAWYER: So is that what you're doing? Pretending not to know about him?

(Pause)

BUSINESSMAN: Look, I just want you to realize that when we've done this, you and I, a few times, that will be that. Michael-and-Michael is forever.

YOUNG LAWYER: *(Feebly)* Didn't you hear me say I love you?

BUSINESSMAN: No. *That's* what I can't afford to do: hear you saying that sort of thing. Kiss me goodbye.

YOUNG LAWYER: *Au revoir*: you'll be back. A few times. Which is better than no times.

*(*BUSINESSMAN *kisses* YOUNG LAWYER *on the lips. The latter makes a feeble attempt to make it a long kiss.)*

BUSINESSMAN: You're very cute, you know that?

(He leaves. YOUNG LAWYER *lifts up the bed and replaces it in the wall.)*

YOUNG LAWYER: *(Sadly)* So who said I'd never make it with a married man?

5
The Businessman and the Lover

(Bedroom of a brownstone in Harlem. Elegant in Victorian style. Late evening. BUSINESSMAN *in bed reading. Enter his* LOVER *in bathrobe. He is white, sixty-ish, somewhat distinguished.)*

BUSINESSMAN: *(Without looking up)* Stopped work, Michael?

LOVER: Yes, I'm tired, Michael. Besides...

BUSINESSMAN: Yes?

LOVER: I was lonely, Michael. For you.

BUSINESSMAN: Is that true, Michael?

LOVER: Can you doubt it? Can you doubt *me*?
Don't read tonight.

BUSINESSMAN: *(Closing the book)* What's up?

LOVER: *(Fervently)* I love you!

BUSINESSMAN: *(Routinely)* I love you.

LOVER: I'm *in* love with you.

BUSINESSMAN: Ah yes. One might forget it sometimes.

LOVER: One has to forget it sometimes.

BUSINESSMAN: Huh?

LOVER: If one didn't forget it sometimes, it wouldn't
be true other times.

BUSINESSMAN: Ah yes, our life style.

LOVER: Our *modus vivendi*. It's provided a score of love
affairs with each other. If we'd just tried to prolong
Affair Number One indefinitely, we'd have been all
through in six months.

BUSINESSMAN: Five.

LOVER: Five and a half. Isn't everyone we know all
through by now?

BUSINESSMAN: All through, twenty times over.

LOVER: By now, you and I would have had nineteen
other lovers each.

BUSINESSMAN: Yeah. But for your great invention.

LOVER: Repeated re-marriage. After periods of being
just friends.

BUSINESSMAN: The let's-just-be-friends routine.

LOVER: Not routine. It's a necessary phase. What you
seminarians call a Retreat. After Retreat, Return.
Re-marriage. One honeymoon after another!

BUSINESSMAN: You couldn't have Number Twenty-One on your mind right now?

LOVER: Frankly, Michael, I can't wait to be your lover—your spouse—once again. This system works like a charm.

BUSINESSMAN: Provided I fit in.

LOVER: You always fit in.

BUSINESSMAN: But supposing, one day, it's just a suppose, supposing one day I wasn't ready at the moment chosen by you. What happens at that moment in the remote future when one day, just by chance, I don't fit in?

LOVER: You'll always fit in.

BUSINESSMAN: Fit in what? It sounds so anatomical. *(Pause)* Sorry.

LOVER: You naughty thing. You're irresistible.

BUSINESSMAN: That's the kinda remark a guy likes to hear.

LOVER: My innocent little seminarian!

BUSINESSMAN: My guilty old capitalist!

LOVER: My generation will never get over its guilt feelings. The whole gay thing being taboo, we had to pick up sex where we could find it.

BUSINESSMAN: And where could you find it?

LOVER: I've told you a hundred times.

BUSINESSMAN: I like hearing it.

LOVER: Subway johns. Turkish baths. The shower room at the Y. The men's room at Bloomingdale's. Or Hunter College, the ninth floor. D'you realize even now what we had to resort to?

BUSINESSMAN: Tell me. I do like hearing it. Who did you have to resort to?

LOVER: Hustlers. Young men driven to whoring by poverty, I suppose.

BUSINESSMAN: I love the way you say "poverty, I suppose"! From on high. Rich bastard.

LOVER: Michael! Being what you call rich doesn't stop me feeling...compassion.

BUSINESSMAN: Do they need it?

LOVER: Hustlers?

BUSINESSMAN: In the seminary, I got to envying people who *have* the pleasures we did without. Especially if they could make a living at it.

LOVER: Michael!

BUSINESSMAN: Michael! I ask you, as the expert. You *used* hustlers and, as you say, I didn't.

LOVER: The big thing is that since we joined forces, we exclude other men. *In* fact and *on* principle.

BUSINESSMAN: Which means it's quite harmless for you to regale me with your, urn, pre-marital amours.

LOVER: There was no *amour* about it. Just lust. With high risk of venereal disease.

BUSINESSMAN: Which you got. Repeatedly.

LOVER: May it be a warning to you, my dear Michael!

BUSINESSMAN: Right you are, my dear Michael. But you've never told me about the fun part. There must've been a fun part.

LOVER: There wasn't.

BUSINESSMAN: Not even for *them*.

LOVER: Least of all for them. Where's the fun in
certainly being poor and probably getting V D?
But let's start up that honeymoon, Mike, please!
I'm horny as hell!

BUSINESSMAN: One question first. Were *all* those
boyfriends—

LOVER: Sex partners—

BUSINESSMAN: Okay, were *all* those sex partners
hustlers? Were they all even promiscuous?

LOVER: What are you getting at?

BUSINESSMAN: Didn't you ever have the experience
of sleeping with a, well, with a monogamous person,
a real life 'spouse'?

LOVER: A gay married man—cheating on his spouse—
with me?

BUSINESSMAN: Exactly.

LOVER: I'd have to decline such a proposition.
It would make me an adulterer.

BUSINESSMAN: *Did* you decline it? Begin again.
If *I* had such an experience, would I be having an
experience you never had?

LOVER: What a funny question! But yes, there was
one guy with a lover—before I met you of course—

BUSINESSMAN: Where is he now?

LOVER: He's dead. I sometimes think such people
always die young

BUSINESSMAN: Lovers?

LOVER: Lovers who cheat on, um—

BUSINESSMAN: Their lovers?

LOVER: Adulterers.

BUSINESSMAN: Drop dead? Just like that?

LOVER: Fast or slow, yes, they die.

BUSINESSMAN: Fast or slow, we all die. What are you doing over there?

LOVER: I'm about to turn the light out. *(And he has his hand on the switch.)*

BUSINESSMAN: So you did have the experience. Now tell me—

LOVER: Let the dead bury their dead, Michael.

BUSINESSMAN: He didn't bury you. What did you make of it? I bet you had a ball.

LOVER: The memory of all that is completely *blacked* out by—

BUSINESSMAN: Your black seminarian?

LOVER: *(Nodding)* And I'm all excited because we're back together again. Honeymooning yet again. Husband! Wife! Black Beauty! Throw back the bedclothes!

(The overhead light goes out.)

* * * * *

(They are still in bed. Bedside light)

LOVER: Lost in thought, Michael?

BUSINESSMAN: Sort of.

LOVER: Penny for them.

BUSINESSMAN: *(Singing)*
Night and you and blue Hawaii
The night is heavenly
And you are heaven to me...

LOVER: *(Who has joined in the song)* Waikiki Beach. Our first honeymoon.

BUSINESSMAN: That's how it should be—all the time.

LOVER: Only it can't be. Read history. Read fiction. Just live.

BUSINESSMAN: It was that way tonight.

LOVER: First night of a honeymoon. First night of our twenty-first honeymoon.

BUSINESSMAN: Tell you what, Michael. Let's drop those just-let's-be-friends periods.

LOVER: What?

BUSINESSMAN: Just drop 'em. Beginning now! Let's not have our twenty-first let's-be-friends period!

LOVER: We're not *gonna* have it. Yet.

BUSINESSMAN: But the time will come.

LOVER: Life is life. And we have the best "arrangement" possible.

BUSINESSMAN: One teeny-weeny question. In the friendship periods, Michael, does your eye wander—once in a while?

LOVER: I thought we disposed of that question long ago. *You* learned the answer in the seminary. Self control. Mind on higher things. I learned it in the world. Work. Lose oneself in work.

BUSINESSMAN: In theory.

LOVER: And practice. So your eye wanders. Must you wander with it?

BUSINESSMAN: Well, do you wander with it?

LOVER: Who did you meet today?

BUSINESSMAN: What?!

LOVER: You've met someone. I can tell.

BUSINESSMAN: Only a lawyer. Someone I thought might handle our real estate.

LOVER: Was he gorgeous?

BUSINESSMAN: He was...okay.

LOVER: Young?

BUSINESSMAN: My age.

LOVER: I'd rather stay with old Lester.

BUSINESSMAN: I'll introduce you to Alex anyway.

LOVER: He doesn't have a last name?

BUSINESSMAN: You're changing the subject.

LOVER: From what?

BUSINESSMAN: When your eye wanders, do you wander with it?

LOVER: I lose myself in work. (Pause) All I want is to settle down. (Pause) With you here, what else *would* I want?

BUSINESSMAN: With your thing for Blacks and all. Younger Blacks.

LOVER: And you're the perfect younger Black.

BUSINESSMAN: Then again you had the hots for teenagers. White teenagers.

LOVER: Before the Flood.

BUSINESSMAN: How d'you feel today when a beautiful white teenager crosses your path?

LOVER: You're teasing me. Because you met a lawyer who was young and...okay.

BUSINESSMAN: I give up.

LOVER: What?

BUSINESSMAN: I'm sleepy. We did have sex.

LOVER: And wasn't it great? A successful marriage in a beautiful home-we have what America wants—we're a success. Till death do us part. Fidelity till Hell freezes over. We made it, didn't we, Michael?

(BUSINESSMAN *is beginning to snore gently.*)

LOVER: My God, he's asleep. *(To himself)* But we did make it. Didn't we?

6
The Lover and the Teenager

(A private dining room in the rear of the Lavender Lounge in SoHo. The door is open. The LOVER *is on a sofa sipping wine. At a small table sits the* TEENAGER *eating a large banana split.*

TEENAGER: Mm!

LOVER: Sounds good.

TEENAGER: Mm!

LOVER: Like another?

TEENAGER: *(Shaking his head)* This is my second after all.

LOVER: Your glass is empty. *(He fills it.)*

TEENAGER: No more wine or—

LOVER: Or what?

TEENAGER: I'll get really drunk, sir.

LOVER: You must call me Randy.

TEENAGER: Is that your name?

LOVER: Of course.

TEENAGER: Mine's Tommy.

LOVER: Hi, Tommy. If that's your name.

TEENAGER: Why wouldn't it be?

LOVER: Then: Hi, Tommy.

TEENAGER: Funny to say "Hi" after all this!
(He motions towards his plate, now empty.)

LOVER: "All this" being a banana split?

TEENAGER: Two banana splits. In...a place like this.
Guess you think I'm pretty cheap.

LOVER: What?

TEENAGER: Letting you pick me up on the sidewalk.

LOVER: I didn't 'pick you up'.

TEENAGER: Well, we got to talkin', an' you said,
"Let's go to an ice cream parlor". This is not an ice
cream parlor.

LOVER: This, you see, is more appropriate to my
situation in life.

TEENAGER: Which is what?

LOVER: I'm what they call a man of means.

TEENAGER: Means means money? Well, this place
is "appropriate" to sump'n else.

LOVER: I beg your pardon?

TEENAGER: This place is gay.

LOVER: You know the neighborhood?

TEENAGER: I can read.

LOVER: Ha?

TEENAGER: It's called the Lavender Lounge, for Pete's
sake.

LOVER: Ah yes.

TEENAGER: But don't worry. Some of my best friends
are gay.

LOVER: How about yourself?

TEENAGER: An' how *about yourself*? Are you a pederast?

LOVER: Wow.

TEENAGER: A pedophile? Bringin' me here an' all?

LOVER: Since you ask: no.

TEENAGER: You just happen to like *me*?

LOVER: That's more like it.

TEENAGER: Not a married man by any chance?

LOVER: Oh, no.

TEENAGER: Or "married" to a guy?

LOVER: *(Nervously)* No, no. Just a lonely bachelor looking for love. L-O-V-E.

TEENAGER: I've heard of it.

LOVER: And you're gay or you wouldn't have come here with me.

TEENAGER: Why not? It's cold out. *(Pause)* An' I didn' know about these private rooms. *(Pause)* So I'm gay. What else is new? I *think* I'm gay. I don't find myself goin' for girls.

LOVER: You like older guys?

TEENAGER: You're an older guy and I've come here with you, haven't I?

LOVER: When did you catch on I was following you?

TEENAGER: Lotsa guys follow me.

LOVER: What do you say to them?

TEENAGER: Nut'n.

LOVER: So I'm privileged.

TEENAGER: You don't scare me. Sump'n tells me you're harmless and, after all, in New York, that's Topic A.

LOVER: You can take care of yourself, then?

TEENAGER: I hope so. And, right now *I'm* privileged, livin' off your ice cream.

LOVER: Not to mention my banana.

TEENAGER: Don't talk dirty.

LOVER: Since you're so sophisticated, couldn't we talk dirty? Together? —Unless you want more ice cream?

TEENAGER: No, thanks. *(Pause)* I never talk dirty. Don't dig it.

LOVER: Like to talk serious then?

TEENAGER: Sure. Though I thought I'd be going soon. I like you, of course, or I wouldn't have come. Wouldn't have spoken to you on the street. But I gotta get back home. *(He stands up.)*

LOVER: Sit down, Tommy.

(TEENAGER hesitates.)

LOVER: The door's wide open. Those that want can leave.

TEENAGER: *(Sitting)* Well, just for a minute.

LOVER: Look, Tommy, am I grabbing your balls? Ripping your clothes off?

TEENAGER: 'Course not. But don't talk like that.

LOVER: Then tell me about yourself.

TEENAGER: Whadda you wanna know?

LOVER: You're gay. You like older guys. Are you... experienced?

TEENAGER: Nah. Just explorin'. I lied to you, Randy. I did know about this place. I hang out on the block. 'Cause my kinda *guys* hang out on the block.

LOVER: Well! I'd say you're pretty damned experienced for—how old are you?

TEENAGER: Fifteen.

LOVER: You're jail bait, Tommy, you know that?

TEENAGER: Sure I know that. An' *I* could be sent to reform school.

LOVER: So you gotta be very careful.

TEENAGER: I *am* very careful, didn't you notice?

LOVER: How many...older guys have you...been with?

TEENAGER: Millions.

LOVER: Seriously?

TEENAGER: Nah. Just a couple. Nine or ten.

LOVER: One night stands?

TEENAGER: One *hour* stands. Ten minute stands. Do it and run.

LOVER: You wanted more?

TEENAGER: With one I did. You remind me of him, you know that?

LOVER: Really? That's very significant, Tommy. And rather wonderful. I remind you of someone. In what way?

TEENAGER: Oh, I dunno. The eyes, I guess. The way you smile.

LOVER: That's very interesting. Even uncanny.

TEENAGER: It is? Uncanny?

LOVER: *(Heavily)* Because you remind *me* of someone.

TEENAGER: And that's significant too? Who may *he* be?

LOVER: Someone your age.

TEENAGER: Your boyfriend? You must introduce me.

LOVER: I can't, Tommy. He's dead.

TEENAGER: Dead? At my age?

LOVER: The good die young. That's a saying.

TEENAGER: A saying that makes me glad I'm bad.
Sorry: I don't want to hurt your feelings, Randy.

LOVER: What was *he* called? The guy you liked.

TEENAGER: I never found out.

LOVER: You...went all the way with him and never
found out his name?

TEENAGER: I found out he was married. And faithful.

LOVER: Except that night.

TEENAGER: Evening. There was my mother to think of.

LOVER: You live with your mother?

TEENAGER: *(Nodding)* She teaches at Queen's College.
That's where my Dad—my late Dad—used to teach

LOVER: What d'you tell her when you get home late?

TEENAGER: She don't ask. *(Pause)* You're pretty nosy,
you know that?

LOVER: I'm interested in you.

TEENAGER: She knows I'm gay, my Mom. She says my
life is mine to live.

LOVER: Sounds terrific, your Mom. Your life is yours
to live. And I'm interested in you.

TEENAGER: You guys sure know what you want. Me,
I decided that night, after that night, not to be in such
a hurry. Learn to take my time. Get hurt less.

LOVER: You got hurt—already?

TEENAGER: Are you kiddin'? It *always* hurts. Afterwards.

LOVER: After—sex?

TEENAGER: Yeah. They all want it. But, when they've
had it, they don't want you.

LOVER: And that hurts, eh, Tommy? How lucky you
are to meet me!

TEENAGER: Don't say you love me.

LOVER: Love's what I'm looking for, I told you that!

TEENAGER: It's too fast.

LOVER: Love at first sight? It happens. It has happened
since the world began.

TEENAGER: It doesn't last.

LOVER: *(Earnestly)* Tell me about the guy I remind
you of, Tommy.

TEENAGER: *(Hand to head)* Your wine's getting to me,
Randy. *(Pause)* He was the same age as you, too.
How old *are* you, thirty?

LOVER: *(Who is obviously quite a lot older, rotates his hand)*
Give or take, um—

TEENAGER: Now I *must* go. *(He gets up with an effort.
It's no good. He sinks down again.)* Did you put something
in that wine?

LOVER: Certainly not. *(Pause)* Ready now?

TEENAGER: The waiter can come in at any moment.

LOVER: No waiter's gonna come in here. Not in your
lifetime.

TEENAGER: Well, at least shut the door. You've worn me
down, Randy boy, you've worn me down.

* * * * *

(The TEENAGER *is spread out on the couch with his eyes closed. The* LOVER *is pacing the room, smoking. Silence)*

LOVER: Done it again. One day Michael will get wind of these things and leave me.... And who *is* this young punk? The creatures one resorts to! How'd I get mixed up with a fifteen-year-old?

TEENAGER: *(Without opening his eyes)* You did put something in that wine.

LOVER: *(Nervously)* What's that? What did you say, Tommy?

TEENAGER: *(Opening his eyes and not seeing* LOVER *at first)* Where are you, Randy? Oh there. Why so far away? Come over here.

*(*LOVER *sits gingerly on the end of the sofa.)*

TEENAGER: You like me, don't you?

LOVER: Isn't that rather obvious?

TEENAGER: What did you put in the wine? Huh? Because, otherwise, I would never...you know...

LOVER: But you did. Because I reminded you of...him.

TEENAGER: Because you got me drunk.

LOVER: Anyway I didn't believe that story.

TEENAGER: Why not?

LOVER: Gay people always lie. Fabricate. Fantasize. The one guy. The one night. "You remind me of someone!" "The eyes, the eyes!"

TEENAGER: The good die young and all that. He reminded you of me.

LOVER: Okay. I lied. *You* lied.

TEENAGER: Only I didn't.

LOVER: Prove it.

TEENAGER: How'd I prove it? Don't nag me.

LOVER: Cigarette? But you're too young, aren't you?

TEENAGER: Yes.

LOVER: My God! D'you realize what time it is?

TEENAGER: What time is it?

LOVER: Twenty five to twelve.

TEENAGER: Why did you want me to know?

LOVER: How about your mother? Or is she a lie too?

TEENAGER: You want me to go?

LOVER: Now that's not fair. You told me yourself that—

TEENAGER: Hey, you're different now.

LOVER: I'm not different at all. At my age a man can't change- not in half an hour!

TEENAGER: I did know about the private dining rooms. But I never went to one. Till tonight. That should show *something*.

LOVER: You know: I think we should have an arrangement, you and I.

TEENAGER: Arrangement?

LOVER: Come here- at certain times, I don't *always* have time—or somewhere else if you don't like this place— what d'you think?

TEENAGER: You still want me—after, urn—

LOVER: I'm looking for love, I told you that.

TEENAGER: But then you wanted me out of here. And when I woke up just now, you were mumbling to yourself that—

LOVER: Post-coital discouragement.

TEENAGER: Post wha-a-t?

LOVER: It doesn't last. When shall I see you next?

TEENAGER: Well, um...

LOVER: Now I don't live in the city.

TEENAGER: You commute?

LOVER: No, no, I live...in the country.

TEENAGER: Like where?

LOVER: Does it matter?

TEENAGER: Don't worry, I won't come out there and surprise you!

LOVER: You can come out as much as you want! I live in Westchester.

TEENAGER: *(Sceptically)* Yeah?

LOVER: A lot of people live in Westchester!

TEENAGER: I recognize the symptoms: you're married. And you probably live about two blocks from here.

LOVER: Well, I'm not exactly married. What made you think I was?

TEENAGER: You don't live in town and don't always have the time.

LOVER: You're smart.

TEENAGER: Experienced. You said I was. And take this: you're not "exactly" married. You're *inexactly* married?

LOVER: I didn't say that.

TEENAGER: It means you have a lover. You're married to *a guy*.

LOVER: Now don't start feeling bad because you think you've broken into a marriage.

TEENAGER: That wouldn't make me feel bad. Married guys *want* their marriages broken into. Where is your lover right now? *(Tauntingly)* Somewhere like this? Or at the Baths?

LOVER: Cut it out! That's in really bad taste.

TEENAGER: I thought you didn't have a lover?

LOVER: Whether I have a lover or not, such remarks are—

TEENAGER: Randy!

LOVER: Tommy!

TEENAGER: You're mad at me. Don't be. So you're not married and you don't have a lover. Can we be friends?

LOVER: You're a terrific guy, you know that? Let me hold you. Just for a second.

(He not only holds him but runs his hands over him urgently.

TEENAGER: Oh, no, not again, it *is* late.

LOVER: Okay, sit down. I won't touch you. *(And now he doesn't.)* We must have a serious talk. Tommy, I want to see you again. And again. And again.

TEENAGER: I'll believe that when I see it.

LOVER: Tommy, you're forgetting—

TEENAGER: You're lookin' for love—?

LOVER: Okay. I'm not looking for love. I do have a lover, and I love him.

TEENAGER: Does he know you sleep around?

LOVER: I don't.

TEENAGER: Ha?

LOVER: Well, not much.

TEENAGER: "Again and again and again."

LOVER: That's three times.

TEENAGER: I suppose he does likewise "again and again and again". Three times.

LOVER: No, he doesn't.

TEENAGER: He *says* he doesn't.

LOVER: I know he doesn't.

TEENAGER: How can you be sure?

LOVER: I just am.

TEENAGER: Really?

LOVER: Even if I weren't, I'd pretend I was.

TEENAGER: Well! In *that* case

LOVER: Look. Can we change the subject?

TEENAGER: Sure. I've been coming to certain conclusions.

LOVER: You *are* a big boy.

TEENAGER: I guess I *am* lookin' for love.

LOVER: What?

TEENAGER: Okay, I like older guys. I enjoy sex. With you, fr'instance. But I want more. I gotta find someone to *give* me more.

LOVER: Looking for Mister Right?

TEENAGER: What's wrong with Mister Right? You have your Mister Right and aren't about to give him up for the likes of me.

LOVER: I didn't call you the likes of you.

TEENAGER: You're sweet. *(Pause)* But I'm gonna split.

LOVER: Forever?

TEENAGER: It *is* a long time. But you can take care of yourself. Should I wish you good hunting? Or a happy marriage?

LOVER: Oh, both, both, by all means.

TEENAGER: 'Bye, then.

LOVER: Just like that?

TEENAGER: Like this. (*Walks over to him, kisses him on the lips.*) 'Bye again.

(*He leaves. The* LOVER *watches him go, then walks to the door.*)

LOVER: Waiter! My check!

7
The Teenager and the Writer

(*Spacious studio apartment on West End Avenue done up to look Gothic: even the one window we see has a paper maché Gothic arch in front of it. Desk. Papers. It is rather dark. The* TEENAGER *and the* WRITER *come in. The* WRITER *carefully locks the door behind them. There is enough light for us to see that the* TEENAGER *is wowed by the Gothic effect.*)

WRITER: Well, such is my modest pad. The throne room, if you will. It's the only room actually. Now kiss me. (*He snatches at the* TEENAGER *in an enthusiastic embrace. Letting him go.*) Phew! I've waited for that! Through three long hours of Central Park!

TEENAGER: It's so dark in here.

WRITER: Gothic gloom. Romantic, ha?

TEENAGER: Can we have some light now?

WRITER: No. My interior decorator expressly forbids it. Officially, we don't even *have* light.

TEENAGER: But you're a writer, aren't you? When you write—

WRITER: Oh, if I work at night, I may smuggle in a flashlight. There may even be a little switch—behind the arras. *(He points to a drape.)* But when I play, I play in the dark! Or by candlelight. I have long slender church candles. Lewd, huh? Another little kiss.

(He again kisses TEENAGER *on the lips.* TEENAGER *accepts but does not react.)*

TEENAGER: Now I gotta split. Thanks for showin' me your pad. It's great.

WRITER: We only just arrived.

TEENAGER: Like I said. I can only stay a minute.

WRITER: Oh, look. *(He looks at his rug which* TEENAGER *is standing on.)* You must take your shoes off.

TEENAGER: For one minute?

WRITER: For my one and only Persian rug. Gift of the Shah.

TEENAGER: You know the Shah of...is that Iran?

WRITER: Gift of the Shah to...a friend of mine. With Persian music to match.

(He plays a tape of In a Persian Market *by Ketelby. The music continues softly behind the following dialogue.)*

WRITER: Lie down, my pet, while I recite a poem. One of my own.

*(*TEENAGER *turns in surprise.)*

WRITER: Yeah, you gotta lie down for this. It's a Persian custom.

*(*TEENAGER *lounges on a divan.)*

WRITER: Flat on your back. With your eyes closed.

*(*TEENAGER *obeys.)*

TEENAGER: *(From the position indicated)* Did you say a poem of your own?

WRITER: *(Lighting a candle)* Is that what I said?

TEENAGER: I thought you wrote plays?

WRITER: I, er—

TEENAGER: You're not famous, are you? You said, one of my own.

WRITER: If a poem is good, who cares who wrote it?

TEENAGER: No one, I guess.

WRITER: You don't know what I'm talking about, do you?

TEENAGER: Maybe not. *(Looks at the divan)* I could doze right off on this thing.

WRITER: *(Seated and writing by candlelight in a notebook)* "...has no idea what I'm talking about. *Sancta simplicitas.*"

TEENAGER: *(Overhearing this last phrase)* That's not English, is it?

WRITER: Not quite.

TEENAGER: I bet it's derogatory. About me.

WRITER: *Au contraire.* It celebrates your divine simplicity.

TEENAGER: In other words, I'm dumb.

WRITER: That's all right. You're beautiful. And young.

TEENAGER: And you have the brains. And maturity.

WRITER: "But the myrtle and ivy..." How old did you say you were?

TEENAGER: Fifteen.

WRITER: "The myrtle and ivy of sweet fifteen
Are worth all the laurels that ever have been."

(*TEENAGER's eyes are closed.*)

WRITER: Did that put you to sleep?

TEENAGER: No. Was that your poem?

WRITER: That was Lord Byron's poem. My translation.

TEENAGER: I'm waitin' to hear *your* poem.

WRITER: (*Stroking his hair*) I'm basking in your presence.

TEENAGER: You're ruining my hair-do.

WRITER: (*Again writing*) 'After a day in the spring
sunshine, we take refuge, now, in the Gothic twilight
of West End Avenue, wrapped in its cryptic shadows
as in a—as in a what?

TEENAGER: Are you asking me?

WRITER: I'm in the throes of creation.

TEENAGER: (*Whose eyes have been closed*) Here and now?

WRITER: Of course. I'm improvizing. At your feet.

TEENAGER: You're at my head. I liked your poem.

WRITER: You shouldn't have. It was bad. And it wasn't
my poem. (*He scribbles away.*)

TEENAGER: What are you doing now?

WRITER: Writing about you.

TEENAGER: I'm gonna be in a book?

WRITER: In a play. With luck. With inspiration. I don't
just tape-record people, you understand. I transpose.
I transform. I transfigure.

TEENAGER: You've lost me.

WRITER: Then how about a little something to eat...
to drink...?

TEENAGER: I'm hungry.

WRITER: Be thirsty, do you mind? If it's food we need, I'll have to run out and get it at the deli.

TEENAGER: Any ice cream in the freezer? You do have a fridge?

WRITER: Hidden away someplace, maybe—

TEENAGER: And a couple of bananas?

WRITER: *(Shaking his head)* Look, I'll run out to the deli.

TEENAGER: *(Getting up)* Forget it. I gotta go home.

WRITER: No, no, no, no, no! When we're...ready to leave, we'll have supper out. There's a great Mexican place one block away.

TEENAGER: You and me? We'd get good an' stared at.

WRITER: This is the West Side!

TEENAGER: The West Side would consider you a child molester.

WRITER: Oh, there are places for people in...our position...

TEENAGER: Kids with older guys?

WRITER: And I bet you know all about it, too. You're the type.

TEENAGER: What type?

WRITER: The type an older guy takes to, oh, a private room in the back of some gay bar.

TEENAGER: *(Challenged)* Come to think of it, I *was* taken to some such place once.

WRITER: Who was the lucky guy?

TEENAGER: *(Defiant)* My Mom took me there for my birthday.

WRITER: You sure tell tall stories. I can't see you in this light but I bet you're blushing. *(Moves close to feel his cheeks.)* I can *feel* the hot blood in your cheeks. But, I can't remember, now, what you look like!

TEENAGER: Thanks!

WRITER: *(Very seriously)* It's rather spooky. *(He writes.)* "If I can't visualize your face, it means I've forgotten you." Now say something! And I'll improvise.

TEENAGER: What?

WRITER: Thanks. *(He improvises without writing.)* "You said: 'what', and I did not recognize your voice! I *have* forgotten you! We are a thousand miles apart. A thousand years apart. Yet I only have to light a candle, you return, and I remember you..." Corny, huh?

TEENAGER: I kinda liked that too.

WRITER: You're adorable. May I kiss you?

TEENAGER: You already have.

WRITER: Where are your lips?

TEENAGER: Just above my chin. No, not below my neck. There!

(They kiss.)

WRITER: Something you said in Central Park really touched me.

TEENAGER: "I love you, I love you, I love you...."

WRITER: Yes. Dare I believe it?

TEENAGER: Depends how much courage you got.

WRITER: Well, do you say that to all the guys?

TEENAGER: All the guys on earth?

WRITER: Two or three dozen you might have met.

TEENAGER: Nah.

WRITER: But you said there *was* one.

TEENAGER: He was married.

WRITER: Oh yes. And faithful.

TEENAGER: Except that one time.

WRITER: I don't want you thinking about him.

TEENAGER: You brought him up.

WRITER: Look, are you going to have sex with me?

TEENAGER: Not just like that. No.

WRITER: You aren't on your way out?

TEENAGER: As a matter of fact, I am. *(He gets up.)*

WRITER: At least let me *see* you before you go....

TEENAGER: See me?

WRITER: Hold it. I wanna show you something.

(He takes a photo album from a drawer and gives it to TEENAGER.*)*

TEENAGER: *(Inspecting the contents, taking his time before speaking)* Naked boys, huh? But in real good taste.

WRITER: Classical taste. Neo-Greek poses, see that?

(As TEENAGER *is flipping through, he points to a picture.)*

TEENAGER: Who took these pictures?

*(*WRITER *points to himself.)*

TEENAGER: You? All of them?

*(*WRITER *nods.)*

TEENAGER: Hey, you said you were a playwright! And a poet!

WRITER: Photography's my hobby.

TEENAGER: I can certainly see why.

WRITER: Well, would you object?

TEENAGER: To being photographed like *that*? —Jesus! *(He points at the pictures.)* Think I don't dare? I don't have time. You know that.

WRITER: Just one shot. It'll take all of thirty seconds.

TEENAGER: Thirty seconds to do, yeah. Then in your album forever. Then magazines. Marilyn Monroe calendars... My Mom would pass out.

WRITER: *(Showing his camera, which just happens to be handy)* It's a Polaroid. If I give you the picture, you got the negative too.

TEENAGER: *(Suspicious)* Then what's in it for you?

WRITER: Seeing you. In all your glory.

TEENAGER: Stark naked? I wear bikini underwear. It's *very* photogenic!

WRITER: I dare you!

(Slowly, TEENAGER starts to strip.)

* * * * *

(The studio is now brightly lit—by electricity. The WRITER is getting dressed. Lying on the divan, the TEENAGER is naked.)

TEENAGER: You still haven't taken my picture.

WRITER: That was terrific sex, first things first. What's your name, by the way?

TEENAGER: Tommy. What's yours?

WRITER: Robert.

TEENAGER: So now we know each other.

WRITER: In the Biblical sense, even.

TEENAGER: I like you as it turns out. May I know your last name?

WRITER: I call myself Robert Rich.

TEENAGER: Call yourself?

WRITER: I write under that name, you've probably seen it around?

TEENAGER: I guess I should have. In *T V Guide*?

WRITER: The *Village Voice*. *The New York Times* once in a while.

TEENAGER: Far out. Would I have seen your stuff on the tube?

WRITER: If you watch Public Television. Have you ever been to a theater, Tommy?

TEENAGER: You mean, not the movies? No.

WRITER: I have a play in preview all this week.

TEENAGER: On Broadway?

WRITER: Off-Off Broadway. You must come see it with me.

TEENAGER: Like I said—we'd get stared at.

WRITER: I could get you a ticket by yourself.

TEENAGER: Is it funny?

WRITER: *(Nodding)* Mademoiselle Charlot's in it.

TEENAGER: I've heard of him.

WRITER: Her!

TEENAGER: *(Grimacing)* A real screwball.

WRITER: *(Reaching for his camera)* Pull that face again. I'll take a picture.

TEENAGER: Of *my face*?! I got undressed for that?

WRITER: That face.

(TEENAGER *pulls the face again. The camera flashes.*)

WRITER: You can get dressed now.

TEENAGER: *(Getting dressed during the following dialogue)*
Have I been manipulated, would you say?

WRITER: Depends. Did you like it?

TEENAGER: Sure.

WRITER: Then you weren't. Hey, look at this picture.

(The Polaroid picture comes clear as they watch it.)

TEENAGER: He reminds me of someone.

WRITER: Me too. May I keep it?

TEENAGER: It's not a nude, so okay.

WRITER: When you told me you loved me—

TEENAGER: In Central Park?

WRITER: Yeah, did you notice anything strange?

TEENAGER: Yeah. *You* didn't say you loved *me.*

WRITER: *(Nodding gravely)* I say it now. It took till now!

TEENAGER: Till we'd had sex?

(WRITER shakes his head.)

TEENAGER: Till you'd taken my picture? A head shot?!

WRITER: Till you found out I was Robert Rich.

TEENAGER: I don't get it.

WRITER You hadn't known. You hadn't loved Robert
Rich. You had loved *me.* For myself alone. I might have
been a gas station attendant. You'd have loved me just
the same .

TEENAGER: Only I was kidding.

WRITER: I was suspicious! Let me admit it now. All the
boys want to sleep with Robert Rich.

TEENAGER: *(Grinning)* He offers them such "terrific sex".

WRITER: Stop a minute. You're not a Star Fucker,
are you?

TEENAGER: What's that?

WRITER: Tommy, forget everything I just said.
Forget you ever heard of Robert Rich.

TEENAGER: You forgot me. I gotta forget you now?

WRITER: Hold in your memory the *me* you have
known all these years

TEENAGER: We met today in Central Park.

WRITER: And you said, "I love you, I love you,
I love you". That makes it years.

TEENAGER: Sorry.

WRITER: I'm not a playwright. I'm not a poet. I'm not
a photographer. I'm just a guy who...plays piano...
in a piano bar.

TEENAGER: *(Intrigued) Can* you play the piano?

WRITER: Certainly.

TEENAGER: I like *that* idea. The piano bar.

WRITER: Tommy, can you take a couple of weeks off?
Sometime soon?

TEENAGER: Off school!?

WRITER: You're still in school? How about summer?

TEENAGER: What would I tell Mom? What did you have
in mind?

WRITER: A vacation with you. In a Caribbean paradise.
Palm trees. A beach for two. You've seen the ads in the
subway. We'll become one with nature.

TEENAGER: And afterwards?

WRITER: Death ends all.

TEENAGER: Not just yet, I hope.

WRITER: When the bell tolls, it tolls for thee.

TEENAGER: You're saying that now? The day we met?

WRITER: *(Pacing the room)* Tommy? Is that you? Are you still there?

TEENAGER: Can't you see me now I have my clothes on?

WRITER: Put your shoes on, Tommy.

(TEENAGER does so while WRITER continues.)

WRITER: And tell me something.

TEENAGER: What?

WRITER: Are you happy?

TEENAGER: How d'ya mean?

WRITER: When you confront the world, Tommy— your life, your death—are you happy?

TEENAGER: Things could be better.

WRITER: You misunderstand. No, I haven't forgotten what you told me in the Park. Your Mom's a widow. Queen's College doesn't pay her enough. But, setting all that aside, do you feel alive? *Are* you alive? Are you *real*?

TEENAGER: Got a comb?

WRITER: *(Takes a comb over to TEENAGER)* You are *so* beautiful!

(He embraces him.)

TEENAGER: Your hands are all over the place.

WRITER: Stay a while. I'll go out and get that food and then—

TEENAGER: Robert, it really is too late.

WRITER: Only nine o'clock.

TEENAGER: Which is too late.

WRITER: When shall I see you, Thomas? May I call you Thomas? It'll give you stature.

TEENAGER: Okay, so you're horny. But does it have to be with me? If you're not sure I'm real.

WRITER: Which doesn't mean I don't love you. Or couldn't.

TEENAGER: There's no one else in your life? Lover or whatever?

WRITER: Did I say *that*?

TEENAGER: I'm asking.

WRITER: All Greenwich Village knows about me and...well, have you heard of D'Annunzio and Duse?

TEENAGER: No.

WRITER: Richard Burton and Elizabeth Taylor?

TEENAGER: Sure.

WRITER: Well, that's us, today: Robert Rich and—

TEENAGER: So you *are* Robert Rich?

WRITER: Robert Rich and Mademoiselle Charlot. To sleep with *anyone* else is to betray her.

TEENAGER: But you just slept with me.

WRITER: Oh, I'm not *complaining*. I get my kicks that way.

TEENAGER: From betraying somebody?

WRITER: Sex isn't sex unless someone's being deceived.

TEENAGER: Then, if you and I were going steady, you'd be deceiving me?

WRITER: No, no. You aren't the type.

TEENAGER: The type you deceive?

WRITER: You're the type I deceive *with*. And you loved it. You said it was terrific sex.

TEENAGER: *You* said it was terrific sex. And anyway, I didn't know. So I was deceived.

WRITER: Whadda you want? To change the world?

TEENAGER: I enjoyed what we did but, um—

WRITER: You wanna be Beatrice to my Dante.
"Love is not love
Which alters when it alteration finds
And bends, with the remover, to remove..."

TEENAGER: Robert! Shut up a minute. *(Silence)*
Do you like me?

WRITER: Yes.

TEENAGER: So, if this...liking grew, one day, to be more, you could consider giving her up—for me?

WRITER: *(Vehemently)* But she stimulates my appetite for you!

(TEENAGER recoils.)

WRITER: I take that back. What's *really* real, Tommy? The present moment, huh? Well, right now there is just you. And it's just you I'd like to make another date with.

TEENAGER: Some summer in the Caribbean?

WRITER: Right now. Just stay awhile...

TEENAGER: No, no, you know I gotta split.

WRITER: Tomorrow.

TEENAGER: It's Saturday. I gotta help Mom with the shopping.

WRITER: Sunday then. After the matinee. I'll get you a ticket for the show and see you afterwards. The play by Robert Rich, remember?

TEENAGER: I can't see you afterwards.

WRITER: Later that evening

TEENAGER: Not ever. We just aren't...for each other.

WRITER: I was tactless. I apologize.

TEENAGER: You are you. I'm different, I guess. Dante and Beatrice? Don't know much about *them*. How about David and Jonathan?

WRITER: No role for me in *that* partnership.

TEENAGER: Can I still use the ticket?

WRITER: Of course. It'll be in the box office in my name.

TEENAGER: Robert Rich?

WRITER: *(Nods; a pause, then)* And thanks for everything, kid. Hey, this is the nicest goodbye ever! Thank you!

TEENAGER: *(Turning to go)* Thank *you*, Mister Rich.

8
The Writer and the Actress

(Dressing room of Mademoiselle Charlot in an Off-Off Broadway theatre on Washington Square. The ACTRESS, *in an evening gown and full make-up, is on her knees before a small crucifix. The door opens and the* WRITER'*s head pops in.)*

WRITER: Half-hour, Charles. *(He sees that the* ACTRESS *is on her knees.)* What, in God's name, are you up to?

ACTRESS: In God's name is right. I'm praying.

WRITER: You don't even believe in God.

ACTRESS: Believe in God? I practically own Him. Spent my whole childhood on my knees in the churches of San Juan. Sundays anyway. Kneel with me. Pray for inspiration.

WRITER: We pray standing. We who spent our Saturdays in the synagogues of Brooklyn.

ACTRESS: What are my options? Aerobics? Yoga? Transcendental meditation?

(He has knelt down to cuddle with her.)

ACTRESS: Don't do that. It's blasphemous.

WRITER: Tell God on me.

ACTRESS: I was just telling him all about you.

WRITER: Did he comment?

ACTRESS: He said I'd be a big hit tonight— if only your play holds up.

WRITER: If the play's a hit, it'll hold us both up for months, and you know it.

ACTRESS: That's why we must both pray our hearts out.

(Kneeling still, he pinches her backside.)

ACTRESS: Are you out of your mind? At half hour? On the opening night of a play that, whatever its modest merits, cannot possibly succeed, except as a vehicle for the talents of Mademoiselle Charlot, the greatest female impersonator East of Japan? All there's time for is a little prayer. A little God music.

WRITER: On the opening night of—what was it?—

ACTRESS: How would *I* know?

WRITER: You were known to be fucking Bernie Blossom ten minutes before curtain time.

ACTRESS: Are you still jealous of Bernie Blossom? He's in San Francisco.

WRITER: I'm citing historic precedent.

ACTRESS: I *worshipped* that guy.

WRITER: You told me.

ACTRESS: I'm sorry. I can leave if I bore you.

WRITER: Leave and go where? In that outfit?
At half hour?

ACTRESS: Then you can leave. It *is* more suitable.

WRITER: Look. I know we are Burton and Taylor—

ACTRESS: D'Annunzio and Duse—

WRITER: Accept the adoration of your author, damn it.
Never mind the Author of your being.

ACTRESS: I accept all the adoration I can get. Now leave
me to my prayers! I'll pray for you.

WRITER: You're kicking me out?

ACTRESS: Yeah.

WRITER: Rejecting my...little suggestion?

ACTRESS: How can I fool around with all this on?
(Pause) Oh, very well, tell the stage manager, we go
up ten minutes late tonight and not to disturb me till
quarter hour.

WRITER: So you will—

ACTRESS: Be back in three minutes and keep out of the
other dressing rooms.

WRITER: I'll be on MacDougal Street studying the
masses.

ACTRESS: They're worth *two* minutes anyway. You have
your notebook on you?

WRITER: You bet. *(He displays it.)*

ACTRESS: Keep your hands off the boy in the box office.

(WRITER *leaves. The lights dim. When they come up,*
ACTRESS *is revealed as a youngish man, slightly bald,*
in a bikini. A knock on the door)

ACTRESS: *(Grandly)* Who is it?

WRITER: Three guesses.

(ACTRESS *opens the door.*)

WRITER: It's a boy!

ACTRESS: Lock the door. No, first put the Do Not Disturb sign out.

WRITER: *(Shakes his head)* Then all MacDougal Street will be in on it.

ACTRESS: *(Finger and thumb together)* You're right. Just lock up.

WRITER: Off with that bikini.

ACTRESS: The boy is a gentleman. Sit down beside him, and tell him the secret of eternal youth.

WRITER: *(Beside her as bidden)* And what else?

ACTRESS: Tell him who you are cheating on at this very moment, *mon cher.*

WRITER: I'm not cheating on anyone at this very moment, *ma chère*

ACTRESS: Well, don't fret about it. I am, too.

WRITER: You are, too, what?

ACTRESS: Cheating.

WRITER: I'll bet.

ACTRESS: On whom?

WRITER: It's anyone's guess.

ACTRESS: What's your guess?

WRITER: Oh, our dear, sweet producer?

ACTRESS: How would he have the time for me? He has every boy in the cast coming and going.

WRITER: Our leading man?

ACTRESS: Lenny? He's a flaming straight, didn't ya know? Prowls the *Village* in search of that endangered species, the straight female.

WRITER: Bernie Blossom?

ACTRESS: Don't be rude. I haven't seen him in five years.

WRITER: I give up.

ACTRESS: Okay. Shall we dance?

WRITER: It's now or never.

ACTRESS: What's *that*? That funny little sound? Listen! The crickets are chirping in the park!

WRITER: Crickets on Washington Square?

ACTRESS: Why not? There's grass, there's trees. If you want romance, you got to have romantic atmosphere. Hark!

WRITER: Who says "hark" in the Nineteen Seventies?

ACTRESS: *(Severely)* We drag queens all say "hark" when we're on our high horse.

WRITER: You're not a drag queen, you're a female impersonator.

ACTRESS: A Kabuki Queen.

WRITER: That's why we all love you.

ACTRESS: I suppose you'd like to have an affair with me, Mister Rich?

WRITER: I thought you might realize that sooner or later, Mademoiselle Charlot.

ACTRESS: You'd all like to have an affair with me, you men. You men-men.

WRITER: But at this moment in time the odds are rather strongly in my favor.

ACTRESS: All right, Cricket. I'm going to call you Cricket from now on.

WRITER: So you got your cricket after all.

ACTRESS: Who are you cheating on? Right now. There must be *someone.*

WRITER: A little blond teenager that tracks older guys. His mother teaches at Queen's College. How about you?

ACTRESS: How *about* me? I haven't looked at anything but your damned script for months.

WRITER: And the Virgin Mary. *(He points to the statuette.)*

ACTRESS: She won't even do it with Joseph.

WRITER: That leaves—??

ACTRESS: That leaves nobody.

WRITER: In your past.

ACTRESS: Or present.

WRITER: How about the future?

ACTRESS: That doesn't make sense.

WRITER: Someone you haven't yet met. But you're already planning to cheat on him.

ACTRESS: Cricket, you are talking rot, and we only have ten minutes left.

WRITER: My God, you're right. Listen. Concentrate. There is a man somewhere. The one man in the world that's meant for you. Do you see him—in your mind's eye? Don't answer. You've gone to work on him. Ts, ts, ts, you are cheating on him already!

ACTRESS: *(Weakly)* Already? With who?

WRITER: With who? Who but me, Charlie darling? Me, me, me! *(He starts to move in.)*

* * * * *

(Both are beginning to dress. ACTRESS's *make-up has not been smudged. She will now put her female attire back on.)*

ACTRESS: Well, that's better than acting in damn silly plays, don't you think?

WRITER: Depends on the damn silly play, I should suppose, wouldn't you?

ACTRESS: I know which play you're thinking of....

WRITER: Surprise, surprise.

ACTRESS: Seriously, it's a very great play. You're a genius, Robert.

WRITER: Thanks *(He lights a cigarette.)* Why did you cancel the preview two nights ago? There was nothing wrong with you.

ACTRESS: Oh, just to annoy you.

WRITER: What had I done to deserve it?

ACTRESS: You're so fucking conceited!

WRITER: That's what you think.

ACTRESS: That's what everyone thinks. Everyone who is anyone.

WRITER: Really?

ACTRESS: But I told them

WRITER: Everyone who is anyone?

ACTRESS: Yes. I said: a man like that has every right to be conceited!

WRITER: And what did everyone who is anyone reply?

ACTRESS: How would I know? We're not even on speaking terms. Me and everyone who is anyone.

WRITER: I see.

ACTRESS: They all want me taken care of. You know: shot. By someone in the Mafia. But they will never succeed. I'm hiring bodyguards. Gorgeous bodyguards.

(She is still getting dressed and continues to do so till the end of the scene. WRITER *is dressed again by now.)*

WRITER: Don't think about those people. Just bear in mind I love you, Charlie. Do you love me?

ACTRESS: Haven't I just proved it?

WRITER: Things like that can't be proved.

ACTRESS: Mother ofGod! What more do you want?

WRITER: Do you love all the guys you've had sex with?

ACTRESS: Just one, of course.

WRITER: Well, thanks. You get a little kiss for that.

ACTRESS: I was referring to Bernie Blossom.

WRITER: No. Not tonight! Not right after we—
Then what am I to you, if it's Bernie Blossom you're always thinking of?

ACTRESS: A whim.

(Pause)

WRITER: Well, it's nice to know.

ACTRESS: I think you're quite proud of yourself at that.

WRITER: How so?

ACTRESS: Of your amorous exploits, shall we say? One of them in particular. I can see it in your face.

WRITER: You're seeing stars.

ACTRESS: And hearing crickets. Do you hear them now?

WRITER: Yeah, I hear them.

ACTRESS: Well, that's not crickets, my dear. *(Shouting)* There are no crickets on Washington Square. That's frogs.

WRITER: There are no frogs on Washington Square. Frogs croak.

ACTRESS: I know frogs croak.

WRITER: What I hear is chirping.

ACTRESS: You're pigheaded. Kiss me.

(They kiss.)

ACTRESS: Frog!

WRITER: Don't call me that.

ACTRESS: What *should* I call you? Cricket?

WRITER: I have a name.

ACTRESS: A boring name if ever there was one.

WRITER: *(Simmering)* I am asking you to call me by my name.

ACTRESS: Robert. There! I've called little Robert by his darling little name. Kiss me.

(He does so.)

ACTRESS: Satisfied now—frog? *(A trilling laugh.)*

WRITER: I should take to drink.

ACTRESS: Coke is the thing these days.

WRITER: On Off-Off Broadway earnings?

ACTRESS: Steal it. Bernie does.

WRITER: Bernie! Again! *(Pause)* He actually *steals*?

ACTRESS: By the by, you still haven't said a word about last night's preview.

WRITER: I didn't see last night's preview.

ACTRESS: I suppose that's your idea of a joke.

WRITER: Not a bit. You cancelled the preview before that. You were sick. How could I guess you'd make such a quick recovery?

ACTRESS: Well, you missed something.

WRITER: Like what? A great play? A landmark in the history of American drama?

ACTRESS: I was sensational. People turned pale.

WRITER: You could see the audience?

ACTRESS: Our flaming straight leading man said to me: Darling, you are a goddess.

WRITER: And so sick one day before.

ACTRESS: Know what made me sick? My *yearning* for you.

WRITER: You cancelled that preview to spite me.

ACTRESS: Such a thing as a grand passion is beyond your ken, I suppose. I was running a fever for days on end. My temperature was a hundred-and-five.

WRITER: Quite a temperature—just for a whim.

ACTRESS: How dare you call it a whim, my feeling for you? *(Very loudly)* I'm dying for love of the guy, and he calls it a whim!

WRITER: And Bernie Blossom?

ACTRESS: *(Shrieking)* Don't keep bringing *him* up! The man is a common thief!

9
The Actress and the V I P

(The ACTRESS'*s small but campy loft in SoHo. It is late morning. The bed is made but the* ACTRESS *has not yet dressed. In just a robe, and without make-up, she is propped up on pillows, reading the morning papers.)*

(A ring at the door. The ACTRESS *runs to open it and lets in the* V I P, *a middle-aged man, bald, in an expensive, well-pressed three-piece suit.*

ACTRESS: The spy that came in from the cold! This is an honor, your honor!

V I P: The honor is mine, my dear. I'm not the Mayor of New York by the way. Just a member of your audience last night. You were superb.

(The ACTRESS *offers her hand to be kissed. He kisses it.)*

ACTRESS: You're so kind. I know your face, ofcourse, from the papers. And the tube. What a thrill to see you in the, shall we say, flesh? In my little...boudoir. May I touch? (*With mock reverence, she dares to touch his sleeve.)*

V I P: Am I real? I've often wondered.

ACTRESS: You're a philosopher? I thought of you as a statesman.

V I P: Let's say a public servant. With a large office in City Hall. At heart a student of reality. You were real last night.

ACTRESS: Oh, I'm real *now.*

V I P: I certainly hope so. He looks her over, a new sight to him, without the costume and make-up.

ACTRESS: Do sit down.

(V I P *does so.* ACTRESS *flits about.*)

ACTRESS: I'm so nervous, this being Top Secret and all.
Your man "briefed" me—is that the word? —Yeah,
briefed me about you on the phone. Your name must
never be spoken, etcetera.

V I P: Meaning: don't give me banner headlines in
The Daily News. I pass as straight.

ACTRESS: Well, you're up front anyway, Mister—?

V I P: Call me Henry.

ACTRESS: Prince Hal!

V I P: If you wish. But don't worry about *me*. They told
me you weren't well. Nothing serious, I trust?

ACTRESS: I was dying. Call *me* Charles, Charlie or, when
we're on camera, Mademoiselle Charlot.

V I P: Dying? Not really?

ACTRESS: Very really. But then the show must go on,
as some great Queen once remarked.

V I P: And *how* it went on! Last night was tremendous
and this morning—but I see you have the papers.

ACTRESS: We're a hit.

V I P: A smash.

ACTRESS: Do you recognize me *(Pointing at her present
get-up)* this morning?

V I P: I'm taking you in. This you. It makes
Mademoiselle Charlot all the more wondrous a
creation. How you handled those gowns! And the
spike heels!

ACTRESS: That became...real for you, did it? How about
this? The real little Lord Fauntleroy? Or a mirage of
same?

V I P: A real mirage of same. I like boys too, by the way.

ACTRESS: Even old boys—with thinning hair and a bald patch?

(She shows V I P *her bald patch.)*

V I P: You're still boyish enough.

ACTRESS: And, on stage, girlish enough.

V I P: The original hermaphrodite—Hermes *and* Aphrodite!

ACTRESS: Gender fuck. Pardon the expression.

V I P: Androgyny is the word, I believe.

ACTRESS: Oh, I know, I know, my admirers write books about it.

V I P: I came here to solve the mystery. Learn your secret.

ACTRESS: I'm a Sphinx, Henry? They *were* bisexual, weren't they, those little ol' Sphinxes?

V I P: For the moment, yes, you're my Sphinx.

ACTRESS: How about the boy in the box office?

V I P: How about him?

ACTRESS: For the moment, you like *him*, don't you? The town is talking.

V I P: I've spoken with him.

ACTRESS: Did you...solve *his* riddle?

V I P: Oh, *he's* a Sphinx without a secret. Maybe *that's* why nothing came of it.

ACTRESS: I may be without a secret too.

V I P: Then that will be that, won't it?

ACTRESS: But I *could* be the blue bird of happiness.
In drag. That could be my secret. Wanna know the
secret of happiness?

V I P: I've hunted it at times.

ACTRESS: And love? Dear old love? You must have
searched high and low for that one?

V I P: Very high. And very low.

ACTRESS: But then you heard of Mademoiselle Charlot!

V I P: Yes. Though I'd never seen you till last night. In
my job one doesn't get to the theater, especially not the,
um...

ACTRESS: *Avant garde* theater?

V I P: I realized last night what I've been missing.

ACTRESS: Fun.

V I P: And maybe...another dimension. But Lulu says
I think too much.

ACTRESS: Lulu is quite a name.

V I P: She's my best friend.

ACTRESS: Your fag hag?

V I P: That is not an expression I approve of.

ACTRESS: I shall never use it again.

V I P: Lulu says politicians shouldn't think.

ACTRESS: Lulu must be a real pain in the ass.

V I P: No, no, our work is mindless. And predictable.
All these long meetings. You know exactly what
everyone's going to say. So what's in your head?
Day dreams. Questions. Like: what does it all mean?

ACTRESS: Here you can let it all hang out.

V I P: Do you like people, Mademoiselle? Do you find it possible to like people?

ACTRESS: Certainly not. I loathe them. Which is why you find me alone in a deserted apartment.

V I P: You live by yourself?

ACTRESS: Far from the madding crowd's ignoble strife. They taught us that at City College. A loft in SoHo can be as far from that mad, bad crowd as Antarctica. And much farther than Puerto Rico.

V I P: You're a misanthrope at heart?

ACTRESS: The original misanthrope in the play.

V I P: So am I. Misanthropic, I mean. Is that what draws me to art, Mam'selle? Are artists all misanthropic at heart?

ACTRESS: When they have a heart.

V I P: Unlike politicians, they know why they're alive.

ACTRESS: I haven't a clue why I'm alive.

V I P: You're alive because you have talent. Talent brings recognition.

ACTRESS: And recognition brings...happiness?

V I P: *(Shaking his head)* Happiness is a butterfly. Now you see it, now you don't.

ACTRESS: How about love? Can you catch *that* in your butterfly net?

V I P: Even less than happiness. There are the well-known intoxications, the much-touted ecstasies. Love duets! Love deaths! When the cauldron simmers down, what's left?

ACTRESS: *You* tell *me*.

V I P: Are our young people wrong to accept the intoxication and achieve ecstasy if and as they can? For us today, there is only a present. What is our parents' world, our past? Two world wars, a depression, and a holocaust! We must forget our past. As for our children's world, the future, the population explosion, the polluted environment, the coming holocausts, the coming wars, who dare give them a thought?

ACTRESS: Our "public servants" maybe?

V I P: No, no. When I have a morning off—it *is* still morning?

ACTRESS: Oh, it is.

V I P: Who knows where I may find myself?

ACTRESS: I'm learning.

V I P: I'm learning, too. And politicians don't learn.

ACTRESS: You're a *great* politician I've heard.

V I P: A contradiction in terms, my dear.

ACTRESS: A great lover, then. My John Barrymore. Would you like to take your clothes off?

(He looks startled.)

ACTRESS: Your coat?

(She takes his coat off him.)

V I P: *(Sitting down again)* What were we talking about?

ACTRESS: Everything. Happiness! Dear old love!

V I P: If you can imagine you're in love there'll always be someone to imagine *he* loves you.

ACTRESS: There's always a boy at the box office.

(She tweaks his ear.)

V I P: Charlie!

ACTRESS: The story is all over the Village. You two are a number!

V I P: First I heard of it.

ACTRESS: Well, you did make out, didn't you?

V I P: *The National Enquirer* no doubt says I fought a duel on his behalf and was shot dead.

ACTRESS: *The National Enquirer* is a liar. You are faithful to me!

V I P: What?

ACTRESS: Oh yes. You were faithful to me even before we met. Come closer.

(He sits on the edge of the bed.)

ACTRESS: The boy in the box office belongs to that forgettable past. *(She strokes his head.)* My Prince has a teeny weeny bald patch too.

V I P: Your Prince is all bald patch.

ACTRESS: I knew you were coming, by the way.

V I P: When you got the briefing from my assistant?

ACTRESS: Before that.

V I P: Before that, I hadn't decided to come.

ACTRESS: You were in the front row last night. I played the whole show to just you, saw your face at curtain call, and said to myself: that man will stop by in the morning.

V I P: "Won't you come into my parlor", said the spider to the fly.

ACTRESS: So do something undignified like unbuttoning your...collar.

(He does so.)

ACTRESS: Monsieur Henri, aren't you ever horny?
I mean, you did set this date up. Or did you think it'd
be a philosophy seminar?

V I P: No.

ACTRESS: Then kiss me this minute.

(He administers a long, soft kiss, then returns to his chair.)

ACTRESS: So why'd you stop?

V I P: I didn't 'stop'.

ACTRESS: Henry— Hal—you are *a poseur.*

V I P: How so?

ACTRESS: There's hardly a man in the Village who
wouldn't be happy to be in your shoes.

V I P: *I'm* happy to be in my shoes.

ACTRESS: So happiness does exist! How about love?
Don't you love me, Princeling?

V I P: One might say so.

ACTRESS: Then say it. Say: "I worship you, Charlot!"

V I P: I worship you, Charlot.

ACTRESS: So let your imagination run riot. What do you
want most in all the world?

V I P: Permission to return tonight.

ACTRESS: What?! I'm playing tonight.

V I P: After the theater.

ACTRESS: That's all you want? Nothing else?

V I P: Everything else. But after the theater.

ACTRESS: You are a goddamned poseur, Monsieur
Henri.

V I P: Mademoiselle Charlot, I find you attractive—
to put it mildly

ACTRESS: You put everything mildly, your highness.

V I P: We're going to make love. But why not at leisure,
my dear? At an hour when there are no rings from
doorbell or phone?

ACTRESS: There'll be no rings from doorbell or phone,
idiot. I've taken care of that!

V I P: Sex in the morning is simply not my thing.

ACTRESS: That's an insult!

V I P: It's a compliment, Mademoiselle: one shouldn't
eat a girl like you for breakfast.

ACTRESS: Now that's pretty raunchy.

V I P: I'll be in the back seat, waiting. Not my limousine.
A yellow cab. Not outside the theatre. Two blocks
down. Then somewhere chic for a little supper—

ACTRESS: Champagne, the whole bit? Me still in drag
or what?

V I P: Whichever you like. I like you both ways.

ACTRESS: Hey, now we're gettin' somewhere.

V I P: After which, events will take their natural course.
It will be rather beautiful.

ACTRESS: Gee, it's hot in here.

(All of a sudden he kisses her passionately.)

ACTRESS: Henry! That is not on your program.

V I P: I have no program.

ACTRESS: But it is hot.

V I P: It is *not* hot. That's an old gay gag to get people
into bed.

ACTRESS: So what's wrong with old gay gags?
Take your clothes off.

V I P: I have one last scruple.

ACTRESS: Scruple?!

V I P: Mister Robert Rich...aren't you and he—?

ACTRESS: *(Shrugging)* What if we are?

V I P: You don't mind? What about him?

ACTRESS: Robert? He'll love it. Hearing about you...

V I P: You'll tell him?!

ACTRESS: He's been inventing lovers for me to deceive
him with. You're real, aren't you?

V I P: Comparatively speaking.

ACTRESS: *(Walking over to the Venetian blinds and pulling
them down. As V I P takes his clothes off.)* Antony and
Cleopatra. Tristan and Isolde. Or are you my Romeo?
And are we both thirteen again? Anything is possible.
Finish undressing, your highness. *(She peeps behind the
blinds.)* Night falls over SoHo. This is gonna be a beaut.

* * * * *

(V I P is dressing. ACTRESS is still in bed.)

ACTRESS: So sex in the morning is simply not your
thing. *Poseur!*

V I P: You're a little devil.

ACTRESS: And you're a wonder lover—especially before
breakfast.

V I P: You're the wonder lover.

ACTRESS: And now I should strangle you. Aren't there
insects that do that sort of thing—after sex?

V I P: Oh yes, the—

ACTRESS: And fairy tales about princesses who do it to lovers who learn their fatal secret?

V I P: Yes, indeed, there's one that—

ACTRESS: And how about the prince who learns that the princess has no secret?

V I P: Oh, that would only mean—

ACTRESS: That her secret was just fucking? By whatever name? A fuck by any other name? Antony. Tristan. Romeo. I know what became of *them*.

V I P: They came to a sticky end.

ACTRESS: Which gives me my cue right now.

V I P: For what?

ACTRESS: This line, darling: "I shall never see you again". That's if it's a play. In real life, gay guys are silent. They take down your phone number and fade away.

V I P: Why wouldn't you want to see me again?

ACTRESS: That's not what I said.

V I P: You mean I won't be back.

ACTRESS: I'm not whatever it is you're looking for.

V I P: Maybe no one is.

ACTRESS: So I'm no one.

V I P: I didn't say that. And I didn't say I wouldn't be back...

ACTRESS: So come back tonight. *Then* say goodbye.

V I P: Does that make sense?

ACTRESS: You suggested it. Yellow cab. After the show. Two blocks down the street.

V I P: I see. Well, how about the day after tomorrow?

ACTRESS: By then you'll have forgotten me. Moved on.

V I P: To what? To whom?

ACTRESS: *(Street smart)* Whatsa matter, Mister? Can't do it twice in one day?

V I P: It's no problem physically, Charlie, but let's look at the spiritual side

ACTRESS: I *never* look at the spiritual side!

V I P: I can't separate the two sides.

ACTRESS: If that's philosophy, keep it for your fag hag—what's her name again?

V I P: Lulu. And she isn't a fag hag. Look, Charles, if we don't see eye to eye—

ACTRESS: We'll be eyeball to eyeball. Here! Tonight!

V I P: You insist I come in the yellow cab and—?

ACTRESS: We'll cut the supper and the ridin' around. I'll be back at eleven-thirty sharp. And you'll be waitin' for me, okay?

V I P: It's a crazy little plan.

ACTRESS: One last fuck and goodbye. What's crazy about it?

V I P: So desperate. And the way you word it.

ACTRESS: Wanna call it off? Say g'bye right now? *(Silence)* Which is *more* "desperate": goodbye with a fuck attached, or goodbye and nothin' attached, just nothin' and nothin'?

V I P: I guess we see eye to eye on that one.

ACTRESS: You'll come?

(He nods.)

ACTRESS: Lookin' at the less spiritual side, huh? You know, Mister V I P, Mister Philosopher, Mister

Spiritualist, in your own style you are a very great
seducer! Can you deny it?

V I P: I only meant

ACTRESS: Save it for tonight!

V I P: Tonight?

ACTRESS: Eleven-thirty! Sharp!

(He leaves. ACTRESS is still in bed.)

ACTRESS: Mademoiselle Charlot conquers the
Establishment

10
The V I P and the Hustler

*(A double "room" at the Ansonia Baths on upper Broadway.
Morning, about six. Such rooms have partitions rather than
walls and no furniture other than a double bed and a chair.
No washbasin, no pictures or ornaments. The HUSTLER is
asleep under the bedclothes. The V I P is partially dressed
and on top of the bedclothes just opening his eyes.)*

V I P: "Where am I?" As the heroine says in the
melodrama. Broadway and 73rd. The Ansonia Baths.
Foolish to come here and risk being seen. I must stop
doing these things. *(Looking around)* And, my God,
he's still there, probably glad of as good a place as this
to sleep. I paid him for his trouble. Though, actually,
we didn't do anything. I was too drunk. I must stop
drinking or move from the Ansonia to the Riverside
Funeral Home. Rather nice, to think one can spend the
night at the side of some young fellow, go to sleep, then
kiss him goodbye. Haven't had such a feeling in quite
a while. Must consult Lulu about it. Good boy, that kid.
Kind face now. Not like on the street, brutal, macho.
No one is macho in his sleep. Sleep's a sissy, like his

brother, Death. *Did* we do something, he and I? Nah. Not a thing.

(He has finished dressing and is ready to leave. Evidently the HUSTLER *has followed the last part of this, though he is still more than half asleep.)*

HUSTLER: Hey, you leavin'?

V I P: Oh, hi. Yeah. I gave you fifty bucks last night, remember?

*(*HUSTLER *checks that he still has it.)*

HUSTLER: Oh, yeh, thanks. Don't want nothin' else? I'll sleep some more if that's okay?

V I P: I've had all I want, thanks. What a thing to be able to say: I've had all I want. May I hold you for a minute?

HUSTLER: Hold me all you want.

*(*V I P *goes to* HUSTLER'*s side of the bed and puts an arm round him.*

V I P: What's your name, honey?

HUSTLER: Hyacinth. What's yours, baby?

V I P: *(Impulsively)* Narcissus! Narcissus and Hyacinth! What a pair we make!

HUSTLER: For real? Nar-ciss-us?

V I P: *(The smile fading)* No. In mere reality, things are different, aren't they? In mere reality, one is called Henry.

HUSTLER: You're a big shot, I know.

V I P: What gives you *that* impression?

HUSTLER: Your clothes. And, on the street, you look over your shoulder all the time....

V I P: I'm a middle-sized shot. A little shot, really. How old are you, Hyacinth?

HUSTLER: Eighteen.

V I P: May I ask how long you've been—

HUSTLER: In the business? Two years.

V I P: You started early.

HUSTLER: Better than too late.

V I P: I'm just a student. Of life and such. Tell me something, my dear Hyacinth. Have you ever known... love?

HUSTLER: Ha? Oh yeh. Once. I *think*.

V I P: Tell me about it.

HUSTLER: I really grooved on this guy. Never thought of askin' him for money. Went to sleep in his arms... *(He hesitates.)*

V I P: Yes?

HUSTLER: When I woke up, he was gone.

V I P: Forever?

HUSTLER: *(Nodding)* He was gone. And so was my wallet.

V I P: Oh dear, oh dear. You're unhappy, aren't you, Hyacinth?

HUSTLER: Ha?

V I P: Have you *ever* known happiness?

HUSTLER: *(Defensive)* I'm doin' awright. Did'n' you just give me fifty bucks for... *(He boggles at bad language in front of a V I P.)*

V I P: For nothing. Nothing at all.

HUSTLER: Nah, doan put me down. *That* was more than...a shoe shine, ha? Two years ago I was gettin' fifty *cents* for shinin' shoes.

V I P: You should put *me* down. I pass the time in dreams and idle talk while you struggle for survival.

HUSTLER: I'm doin' awright.

V I P: What do you plan for later?

HUSTLER: Huh?

V I P: When you're too old for...this.

HUSTLER: Whadda they say? "Sufficient to the day..."?

V I P: *(To himself)* "...is the evil thereof." My view exactly. To find people to agree with me I have to come to the Ansonia Baths?

HUSTLER: How's that?

V I P: I'll bother you with another question, Hyacinth, if I may.

HUSTLER: Go ahead.

V I P: Is sex still enjoyable when you... *(He hesitates.)*

HUSTLER: Do it with everybody? But I don't. I'm choosy. I chose you.

V I P: I thought I chose you.

HUSTLER: You're supposed to think that...

V I P: It's all done with mirrors—?

HUSTLER: I choose my guys. Sure, I'll talk with any guy that talks to me. Then—in five minutes—I know if I'm gonna choose him. Chose you in three minutes.

V I P: What did you see in me?

HUSTLER: You're rich. And that counts. Then again, you're real sweet—*under* all that.

V I P: There's a lot of mutual respect here.

HUSTLER: Yeh. You an' me could go places.
In another world.

V I P: My, how strongly you remind me of somebody.

HUSTLER: Oh, please, not that one!

V I P: I know it's a cliché, Hyacinth, but once in a long
while it's true. You have the face of a very wonderful
person I once knew. May I kiss your eyes?

HUSTLER: Why? Then again: why not?

V I P: In memory of him. The eyes are identical.
(He kisses HUSTLER's *eyes.)* And now goodbye.

HUSTLER: 'Bye, Henry.

V I P: One last thing, Hyacinth. Were you surprised?

HUSTLER: At what?

V I P: That we...did nothing. That I didn't ask you to.

HUSTLER: Lotsa guys don't dig morning sex.

V I P: We must do this again sometime.

HUSTLER: Any time. You'll find me...where you found
me last night...where I found you. If you don't, ask the
bartender for Hyacinth.

V I P: *(To himself)* I spend the night with a hustler and
all I do is kiss his eyes because he *truly* reminds me
of someone! Hyacinth, does this happen often?

HUSTLER: What?

V I P: A guy picks you up, pays you, and then doesn't
ask for a thing.

HUSTLER: That has *never* happened. Not in this world.

V I P: Don't take offence. I didn't mean I wasn't
attracted.

HUSTLER: You sure *were* attracted—last night.

V I P: I am now.

HUSTLER: Not like last night.

V I P: Last night I just flopped down on that bed.

HUSTLER: Yeah, with me underneath ya.

V I P: With you underneath me?

HUSTLER: Sure. You don't remember?

V I P: Well, um, not exactly, but, um... Oh dear, is that how it was?

HUSTLER: You must've been really sozzled to forget. You're very good in bed!

V I P: Oh dear... Oh dear. I did pay you?

HUSTLER: *(Letting himself doze off again)* Fifty smackers. Thanks.

(V I P leaves the little room and walks down the corridor.)

V I P: Nice idea, though, to have...just kissed his eyes, there's beauty in it, beauty's the next best thing to love, my dear Lulu, and with love comes the blue bird of happiness...there was *some* resemblance...

END OF PLAY

ROUND ONE/ROUND TWO

Arthur Schnitzler's play REIGEN (ROUND ONE)
was privately printed in 1897 and published in a small
edition in 1903. No such edition of an unperformed
play ever created such commotion. By 1904 sale of this
little book had been forbidden throughout all Germany.
The play was not produced anywhere till 1912, and
then only in a tiny theater in a suburb of Budapest,
Hungary. Performances in Moscow and Saint
Petersburg were reported by German newspapers on
the eve of the October Revolution, 1917, and when, in
the following year, World War I ended, REIGEN was
seen, at lest briefly in smaller theaters, in most of the
great cities of Central Europe, with different degrees
of public outcry and protest. In Berlin, Munich and
Schnitzler's own Vienna, protest led to actual legal
action. Producers and often performers were taken
to court (though they didn't always lose). How far
hysteria could go, and often did, may be suggested
by the following account of a performance in Vienna
on February 16, 1921:

"In the first scene: sharp, penetrating odors caused
by stink bombs. In the fifth scene, a mob of about six
hundred, many of them students, storm the theater.
Ten policemen were unable to stop the onrush. At this
moment, a stink bomb of hydrogen sulfide was thrown
on the floor. The tumult then started. The mob entered,
swinging canes. From the boxes, they hurled paper
balls soaked in tar, eggshells filled with tar, and even

seats, into the auditorium and on to the stage.
Panic ensued. Men trying to defend their escorts
were clubbed, ladies were slapped in the face.
Stagehands hurried to the hydrants, and turned
the hose on the invaders. Soon, stage and dressing
rooms were flooded. The theater was wrecked."

In New York, REIGEN would not get that much
attention but, in the Twenties, it was promptly
confronted by a "Society for the Suppression of Vice".
A translation published in 1920 was to be performed
at The Greenroom Club in 1923 but was downgraded
to a reading by the intervention of that Society. A book
was duly banned, and booksellers who tried to sell it
got arrested. A Court of Special Sessions convicted one
Philip Pesky of Schulte's Bookstore on Fourth Avenue,
holding that the book was "obscene and indecent, being
a lurid study of ten incidents of illicit love relations".
After that, so far as I have been able to discover,
REIGEN didn't make headlines in the United States
until 1950-1 when the French film *La Ronde* was banned
by New York State authorities before being liberated
by the Supreme Court in Washington. The Justices were
shown the film, but found it inoffensive. It remained
highly controversial, however, and was attacked not
only by societies for the suppression of vice, but by
spokesmen for the Roman Catholic Church. Bishop
Joseph F Flannelly of New York spoke of the explosion
of a "moral atomic bomb" that would wreck the moral
standards of the country, and Archbishop John F
O'Hara of Baltimore warned of "poison which can
destroy the soul". Strong words! But it was not 1921,
and New Yorkers would not now respond as the
Viennese had thirty years earlier. How was it with
REIGEN in mid-century America?

Memories of mine may shed light. Preparing my book
The Playwright as Thinker in the early Forties, I had

found Arthur Schnitzler to be one of the great forgotten men of modern drama. None of his plays were on the boards, and to find any of his books I had to go to the secondhand bookshops of Fourth Avenue like the already-mentioned Schulte's. I was so struck by REIGEN that I picked it out from all other Schnitzler plays for inclusion in the first volume of my anthology *From the Modern Repertoire*, 1949. My notes in that volume provided an analysis of it as a comedy... which is to say, as drama, not as pure thought, theory, ideology or whatever. I in no way anticipated what those bishops would say two years later. I wished to revive public interest in Schnitzler and sensed that this would no longer be possible by championing his ideas but only by pointing out his talent, his genius, as an entertainer, as a playwright. What we must bear in mind is that, throughout the twentieth century, public attitudes to sex were in flux. Both world wars loosened things up considerably, and the second world war started a vast cultural shift I will speak of in a moment in connection with ROUND TWO.

In the Fifties I made my own translation of REIGEN, published in my *Modern Theater* series, and got it produced on Sheridan Square by Circle in the Square, ie, Ted Mann and José Quintero. The latter directed it. He had not been shocked by it, nor was he full of missionary zeal as a sexual emancipator. Quintero would later become the great director of Tennessee Williams and Eugene O'Neill. He would make them one with Schnitzler, as he now made Schnitzler one with them. I don't claim that Quintero was influenced by me, only that my wishes did get fulfilled by him. We both spoke of a world much changed, not only from 1897, but from 1921. To a New York theater audience, adultery was no longer shocking, "promiscuity" only mildly so. This was the midpoint of a century at the end of which a girl could go on national T V telling how she sucked the President's cock in the Oval Office....

So, it might be said, "aesthetes" like José Quintero and myself had won out over the social revolutionaries and their banner-carriers. If so, it was a victory without much substance. REIGEN has had quite a few productions since 1955 in more than a few countries, but not only were there no riots, there was also no enthusiasm: no electricity in the air now. And, in theater, electricity is never irrelevant. That the play aroused the anti-Semitic fury of Vienna in 1921 should not be blamed on the anti-Semites, it should be credited to the playwright. What Catholic bishops as late as 1950 could describe as a poison, or as an atomic bomb, was indeed present in REIGEN in the form of a world view quite other than that of the Vatican. Then there is the particular topic of sex to consider. This is a hotter topic in the theater than anywhere else—for several reasons beginning with the actual presence of sexually active bodies on stage in full view. The final sequence of Ibsen's DOLL'S HOUSE has in it all the electricity of the shocking social drama of the era. The husband has asked for sexual intercourse. The wife ends the play by leaving him and their children. With a bang.

The full shock effect depends on how the audience is going to relate to events on stage. At one extreme, they can be bored, and turn away. At the other, they can be outraged and throw stink bombs. The show is only "working" if their reaction is midway between the two extremes. The ending of A STREETCAR NAMED DESIRE provides evidence. The big shock to the audience comes when Blanche tells of her fiancé's suicide. In 1920 this speech would have been cut. In 2007 a New York audience might be shocked by the suicide but not by the homosexuality. The happy medium, I recall, was found in the original premiere

(1947), because the audience was placed, at the time, in exactly the relation to the sex involved that the playwright wished and needed.

In the whole field of sexuality, where, we may ask, changing the metaphor, is the hot button? In the era of Ibsen and beyond, it is in the deviation from the established pattern of fidelity in monogamous marriage and pre-marital abstinence. But in the second half of the twentieth century (not without preliminary flickerings in the first half) there came a great cultural shift. At the center of things now is no longer the adulterer and the fornicator but the bi- and the homo-sexual.

As for me, in 1968-9 I cut a twelve-inch L P under the title *The Queen of 42nd Street*. In its title song I had replaced the heterosexual female of a Jacques Prévert poem with a gay male. In the mid-seventies I wrote LORD ALFRED'S LOVER, a play which is also a mini-bio of the two most famous homosexuals of the late 19th century, Oscar Wilde and Lord Alfred Douglas. It was in the eighties that I wrote a play about gay New York in the seventies: ROUND TWO.

Why, in presenting the late twentieth century, had I glanced back at the late nineteenth when REIGEN (ROUND ONE) was written? The alternative would have been the conventional structure of modern realistic plays from Ibsen to Arthur Miller. The daisy chain of Schnitzler's scenes was eccentric to the point of uniqueness but I was much struck with the way the playwright could swiftly turn from action-before-sex to action-after-sex, and equally from sex-with-one-person to sex-with-another: the battledore and shuttlecock of it was irresistible. I also found myself wanting to take over Schnitzler's highly original handling of the sexual act itself. As modern writers have approached this holy of holies, or unholy of unholies, according to the point of view, they have generally tried to photograph it,

or at least produce rhetoric that will bring the reader
or spectator to orgasm, or almost, along with the
characters. (Think *Lady Chatterley's Lover* either in the
book or in a movie.) What Schnitzler did was: print
a few asterisks, so that the reader skips the physical
lovemaking and its climax and jumps to the
conversation that follows. Technically, what we have
here is the Brechtian alienation effect. We are not *joining
in* with the sex, like teenagers masturbating to a porn
video. We are *watching* what leads to it, and what
thereafter ensues.

So some of what happens in ROUND TWO is what
happened in ROUND ONE. Each character turns from
one partner to another, with much deception, including
self-deception, involved, nor was it hard for the
playwright to provide circumstances in which
characters might make the twists and turns facilitated
by the daisy chain. So far, so good. Beyond this point
ROUND ONE cannot be the model or the guide,
and for one single, overriding reason: the people of
ROUND ONE are hetero-, the people of ROUND TWO
are homo-sexual. For "straights", the norm from which
characters deviated was the "Christian" family, fidelity
within marriage and "purity" before it. Homosexuals,
on the contrary, know no such norm.

One can ask of both ROUND ONE and ROUND TWO,
what is the path that leads from the start of the scene
to the asterisks in the middle? ROUND ONE features
a steady drive toward orgasm, often seduction of a
female by a male. Characteristically, the orgasm is
followed by retreat, at least a calm or boredom, at
worst disappointment and disillusion. ROUND TWO
characteristically features a rather unmoored, lost
person seizing an erotic opportunity and pushing it
all the way to orgasm to see what that might bring
beyond what orgasm has brought, perhaps daily,

in solitary masturbations throughout adolescence.
His orgasms bring no disillusion, for he had
no illusions about them in the first place, but
disappointment? Yes, disappointment that a given
orgasm has led nowhere. Where could it have led?
The homosexual is excluded both from the "Christian"
family and from romantic rebellions against it as
dramatized by Shakespeare in ANTHONY AND
CLEOPATRA (middle aged adultery) and ROMEO
AND JULIET (teenage fornication). In encounters such
as I have tried to present in ROUND TWO people hope,
through orgasm, to break out of their isolation.
Forward, as it were, from solitary masturbation to...
well, what? Maximally, to love, minimally a touch of
friendship, a hint of tenderness.

When I look back now on both plays, I find them in
some ways closer together than I expected. In a crucial
final scene, both plays present an older gentleman
believing he has not had sex with the young prostitute
he is still in bed with after a night together. In both
plays the prostitute has to disillusion him on this score.
In Schnitzler, the older gentleman is comforting himself
with the thought that he has not lowered himself to
the animal levels in this contact with a lower-class and
venal individual, and in ROUND TWO also the older
guy enjoys not remembering the sex he had in fact
reveled in, and he is appropriately crestfallen to be
told how he had actually behaved. But there is further
dramatic action in ROUND TWO of which in REIGEN
there is not a trace. This older gentleman is not in flight
(from respectable sex to sex with the lower orders,
from married sex to adultery) he is pushing forward
into he isn't sure what. Into the unknown then? But
able to reach out to the whore, non-sexually. And since
this whore is not all whore, but is an ordinary New
York boy of gay disposition, the vibrations between

them arrive at much more than just-another-damned-orgasm: tenderness.

ROUND TWO was produced by Celebration Theater of Los Angeles in 1987, and by Wings Theater on Christopher Street in Manhattan in 1991. What I learned from both productions is that the play will not have its proper impact, or even make any clear statement, if it is produced by gay performers for an all gay audience. I don't write plays you can't bring your mother to see, or your daughter, or your teenage nephew. In Los Angeles, word has gone around that my play was a paean to gay sex: Celebration Theater would celebrate sensuality...wasn't there a fuck in the middle of every scene? But, as with Schnitzler, there was a blackout in the middle of every scene and without pause one proceeded to decidedly serious dialogue. REIGEN may well be the saddest comedy ever written. Those Catholic bishops were within their rights to be scared to death. ROUND TWO is further from nihilism and despair, but, for my feeling, deeply sad: the many jokes may, in the end, only make it sadder. And all this was clear in the New York production on nights when the audience was perceptibly general...a family of varied elements, Republican as well as Democratic, the straight as well as the bent.

Review on 27 January 1989 Michael Lassell of the
Los Angeles Herald Examiner

ROUND ONE IS STILL A KNOCKOUT
Bentley's Play is Both Provactive and Challenging

Back in the Gay [18]90s, a gadfly Austrian playwright
named Arthur Schnitzler wrote a play about sex called
THE ROUND or, as it has come to be known in its
French incarnation, LA RONDE. It consists of ten
scenes, each of which described an assignation between
a man and a woman.

The first scene involved a prostitute and a young
soldier; the second portrayed the same soldier and a
parlor maid; the third, the parlor maid and her young
gentleman employer; and so forth. Delightful, satirical
and altogether scandalous, the play could not even be
produced until long after the Victorian era had come
to its end.

ROUND TWO...is the latest of many versions of
the play (there was even a Roger Vadim film starring
Jane Fonda). This one, by world-renowned critic and
playwright Eric Bentley, updates the play to the 1970s,
transports it to New York City and translates the
heterosexual encounters to homosexual ones.

Hence, Schnitzler's "Prostitute" becomes Bentley's
"Hustler", and Schnitzler's "Sweet Young Thing"
becomes Bentley's "Teen-ager", etc. There has been
a lot of necessary adapting to carry off the
transformations, but the revision works and even
manages to incorporate a large slice of Schnitzler's pie.

....

What is most remarkable about ROUND TWO is
not that it draws parallels between heterosexual 1890s
Vienna and 1970s New York—satirically managing
to equate ideas about sex and sex roles with notions
we prefer to consider more enlightened and
contemporary—but that Bentley is able to add elements
of political consciousness about race, class and age
(some of which are implicit in Schnitzler) and pull the
whole thing off as a very funny comedy that is both
streetwise and intellectually stimulating.

Schnitzler himself made a major distinction between
what he called wit—an appreciation of what is
funny—and a sense of the fundamentally comic. "The
comic", Schnitzler wrote, "is denied nothing: not even
when it comes to playing with pain, misery and death.
But permit irony, wit or satire to attempt the same and
it will appear to us as tasteless, crude, if not quite
frankly blasphemous".

There are some, no doubt, who will find any play
about sex, particularly a vernacular play about gay
male sex in which many of the characters are nude
or nearly nude a good deal of the time and everyone
is on the make all the time (although the actual act
is replaced by a moment of darkness on the stage),
to be tasteless and crude. In fact, this production...
is fascinating in its issues, hilarious in its appreciation
of the comedy of life, and an evening of...theater that
is compelling, provocative, challenging and satisfying.
Not to mention an embarrassing bit titillating.

...It is also a play that has as much to say about
heterosexual as homosexual coupling, and one of
the few productions of the play that has ever managed
to make the appeal—or the shock value—of the original
Schnitzler make any sense at all.

www.ingramcontent.com/pod-product-compliance
Lightning Source LLC
Chambersburg PA
CBHW052131090426
42741CB00009B/2035